The *NEW* Knitter's Template

Your Guide to Custom Fit and Style

Martingale®
& COMPANY

Laura Militzer Bryant and Barry Klein

The *New* Knitter's Template:
Your Guide to Custom Fit and Style
© 2010 by Laura Militzer Bryant and Barry Klein

Martingale®
& COMPANY

Martingale & Company
20205 144th Ave. NE
Woodinville, WA 98072-8478 USA
www.martingale-pub.com

Printed in China
15 14 13 12 11 10   8 7 6 5 4 3 2 1

**Library of Congress
Cataloging-in-Publication Data
is available upon request.**

ISBN: 978-1-60468-010-2

Mission Statement

*Dedicated to providing quality products
and service to inspire creativity.*

Credits

President & CEO ✦ Tom Wierzbicki

Editor in Chief ✦ Mary V. Green

Managing Editor ✦ Tina Cook

Developmental Editor ✦ Karen Costello Soltys

Technical Editor ✦ Ursula Reikes

Copy Editor ✦ Sheila Chapman Ryan

Design Director ✦ Stan Green

Production Manager ✦ Regina Girard

Illustrators ✦ Laurel Strand, Adrienne Smitke,
and Laura Militzer Bryant

Cover & Text Designer ✦ Regina Girard

Photographer ✦ Brent Kane

DEDICATION

To knitters everywhere, whose passion
for our craft keeps us motivated

ACKNOWLEDGMENTS

We would like to thank our customers, the retailers, for their enthusiasm and unwavering support of our endeavors, and for promoting us to their customers, the knitters.

A special thanks to "always on call" Ursula, our technical editor. We appreciate that you work hard to make everything we envision possible.

Thank you to our families, whose nurturing love and support made us the people we are.

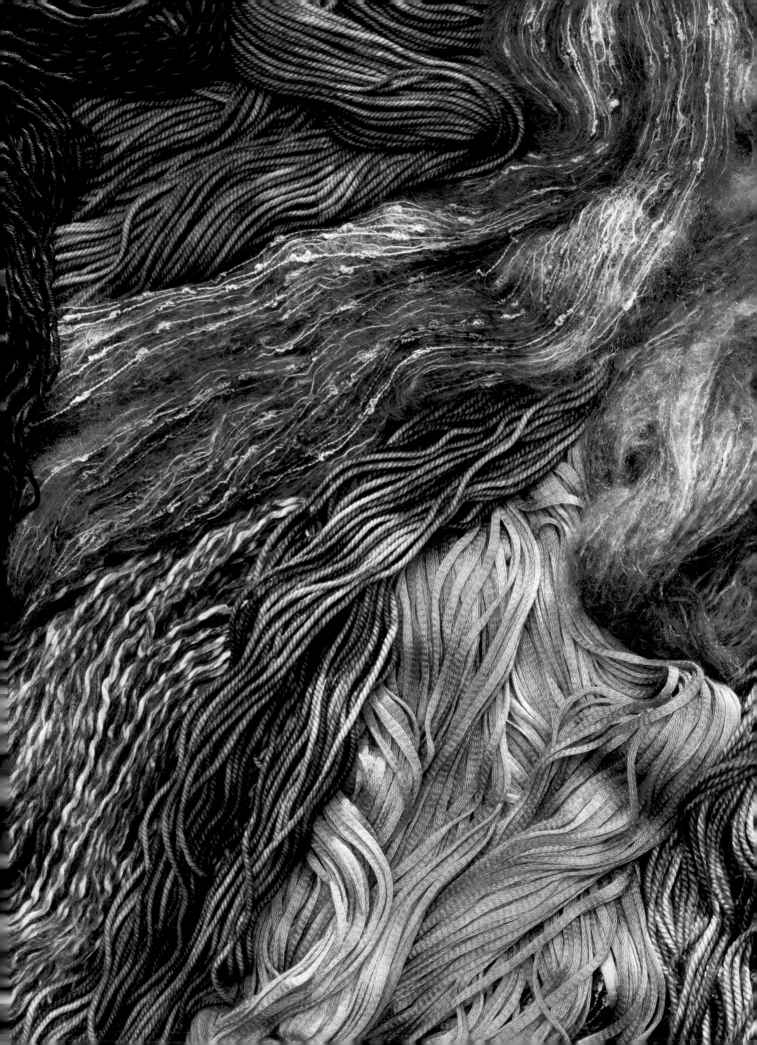

CONTENTS

INTRODUCTION

Welcome to a new adventure. After years of teaching with *A Knitter's Template*, we felt it was time to expand on our original ideas, explore some new ones, and give the book a fresh look. Every day new knitters walk into their local yarn store and seek to make something special. Every yarn-store owner knows the most frequently asked question is for a specific style, gauge, or size of pattern. This book is designed to bring new knitters up to speed and to help move experienced knitters in a new direction, allowing them to knit that envisioned sweater. Whether you have an existing pattern and want to adjust it or you have yarn and want to design something yourself, this book will be your path to success. Our templates, ideas, and passion for knits that fit all come together in these pages, providing you with a knitting mentor.

The templates are designed for a multitude of bust/chest sizes from 30" to 60" and in nine stitch/row gauges. We've given you the numbers and guidance necessary to alter garment shaping to match the lines of your body. The templates in this book cover the most fundamental style: knits worked from the bottom up. Within the basic pieces you can easily work stitch patterns, fair isle, and intarsia color blocks, or knit with textured and self-striping yarns that create designs all their own.

For the templates to work successfully, you'll need to take a full set of body measurements. Yes . . . we did them for ourselves as well. To know your body is to know how to make a garment that fits the way you want it to. As you read *The New Knitter's Template,* you will see tips and answers to frequently asked questions (FAQ) that will help you proceed easily in a confident manner.

Sit back, relax, and surround yourself with your yarn stash. Open the book and let's create some fantastic garments together. You'll be amazed at how easy we've made it for you to design the sweater of your dreams . . . and to have it fit!

USER'S GUIDE

How to Make This Book Work for You

Using a template is easy! Follow these seven steps for a perfect custom garment:

1. Select a yarn and pattern stitch and determine the gauge (page 40).

2. Select a garment type, and then select the styling details (pages 12 and 13).

3. Select the size based on the amount of ease you wish (pages 15–18).

4. Copy the "Blank Pattern Worksheet" (page 28) and "Style Diagram" (page 30).

5. Go to the "Finished Measurement Chart" (page 26) and find your size. Fill in the blank pattern worksheet with the dimensions for your size and style.

6. Go to the templates (pages 66–77) for your stitch gauge and find the column with your size.

7. Following the column down, enter the numbers for your size onto the blank pattern worksheet at the corresponding letters. Make any allowances for borders, pattern-stitch multiples, and adjustments for a custom fit.

Step 1: Yarn and Gauge

Most of us fall in love with a yarn first, and then look for an appropriate pattern. Follow the suggestions in "Feelings: Gauge and Hand" (page 40) to determine the correct needle size and gauge for your yarn. How the yarn feels and acts will help determine which style of garment you choose to make. Soft or limp yarns will not work well for tailored jackets; stiff and heavy yarns may not make the best cropped tops. Consider also how the garment will be worn and how you want it to sit and move on your body. Think about the intended end use—cotton may not make a great ski sweater, while chunky wool doesn't seem right for a summer top. Sometimes, however, the most interesting fashion breaks the rules—menswear styling with a glitzy yarn, or a big cowl-necked sleeveless pullover in fluffy mohair—so don't hesitate to try something different.

You may wish to use a pattern stitch. If so, now is the time to swatch a variety of stitches to find the one you like. See "Changing the Tone: Ten Tricks for Custom Knits" (page 45) for examples of a number of simple stitch and color-work ideas. Stitch dictionaries provide a wealth of patterns. Make sure the gauge is taken over a 4" swatch knit in your pattern stitch! If you're using a stitch with a multiple, record the multiple, plus any edge stitches, on your blank pattern worksheet as well.

Step 2: The Style

The basic template outlined in this book is for garments knit from the bottom up with side seams and sleeves knit separately. Although there are many alternatives to this construction, we wanted to allow as many variations as possible for sizing, fit, and gauge within the space of this book.

Body Lengths

We've included both straight-up and tapered body styles, with five different length options. The desired length will often be a guide for whether to taper or work the body straight.

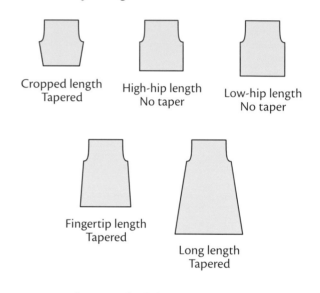

Cropped length
Tapered

High-hip length
No taper

Low-hip length
No taper

Fingertip length
Tapered

Long length
Tapered

- ✦ **Cropped** tops, which hit just below the waist, are usually tapered from a narrower bottom width to a larger bust measurement. This allows the top to sit properly; if it were knit straight up, the hem would tend to stand out from the body, "flapping in the breeze." This length is usually used for sleeveless or short-sleeved summer tops or dressy evening shells.

- ✦ **High-hip** tops, which hit at the top of the hipbone, are generally knit straight up. The high-hip measurement is often similar to the bust measurement, so tapering isn't necessary. This length is good for pullovers or sporty cardigans, whether sleeveless, short sleeved, or long sleeved. A high-hip length allows a smaller circumference than low hip or fingertip, since the garment body doesn't need to accommodate hips and ease. This style is most flattering if the hem just grazes the hips.

✦ **Low-hip** sweaters, which usually cover most of the bottom, must be made with enough ease to accommodate the hips and often taper from a wide hem to a narrower bust. Tapering in this case allows for more ease over the hip, but removes some of the fabric—and thus bulk—before the armhole shaping to allow for a neater shoulder area. Traditional cardigans and oversized pullovers—jackets meant to be worn over slim pants or skirts and most men's garments—are made in this length, most often with straight-up shaping.

✦ **Fingertip** garments reach to the fingers when the arm is relaxed and the fingers slightly curled. Car coats, long tunics, and jackets are worked to this length, which will taper from a wider hem to a narrower bust, or will be large enough to provide ease in the hips. Tapered knitting of this length often hangs better than straight and reduces bulk at the underarms.

✦ **Long** knitted coats or vests can be extremely dramatic. This length will often have taper built in, or it will be sized large enough to provide ease in the hips if made with straight shaping. Even more ease should be allowed for, since longer knitting tends to get heavy, and as it does, it grows even longer and becomes narrower. A long length should be carefully adjusted for the wearer and should include a period of hanging the piece to allow for natural stretch before finishing the armhole and shoulder shaping.

FAQ

I enjoy knitting things in different directions, such as diagonal, side to side, and from the neck down. Can I still use the templates?

The templates are designed for garments knit *from the bottom up*. We have taken into consideration the fit, ease, and style of the many different garment types that can be easily worked in this traditional manner. So although, the style templates can always be used for basic measurements, the gauge/size templates won't be helpful when knitting in a direction different from bottom up. For any type of modular, entrelac, top-down, sideways, or diagonal knitting, work from predetermined measurements, keep a tape measure handy, and check your work often.

Entrelac knitting is not covered in the templates.

Modular knitting is not covered in the templates.

Modular knitting is not covered in the templates but sleeves are.

FAQ: Can I move increases and decreases away from the edges when tapering and shaping body pieces?

We actually *recommend* that you move shaping away from the two edge stitches. Many knitters don't enjoy assembling garments, since the selvages are difficult to read while sewing when increases and decreases are right at the edge. Sometimes designers write instructions simply indicating "full-fashion" shaping. Other designers spell out specifically how to do this. In essence, all shaping can be done one or two stitches from the edge so that once finished pieces are blocked flat, there are continuous edge stitches to follow while assembling the garment. Full-fashioned decreases are most often worked on the third and fourth stitches from each edge, which leaves one selvage stitch for seaming and one stitch between the seam and shaping. They can also be worked on the second and third stitch from each edge, which leaves one selvage stitch for seaming.

It's also important to move your stitches in the right direction by working the correct style of decrease on each side. Look at the direction the needle point faces as you work the shaping stitch to determine which type of increase or decrease is required for the correct slant.

Left-slanting decrease: Work 1 or 2 sts; work 1 ssk (see page 78). Dec slants to left, following selvage edge.

Right-slanting decrease: Work to 3 or 4 sts from edge, work K2tog and finish final 1 or 2 sts. Dec slants to right.

Left-slanting increase (M1L): Insert point of left needle from front to back under thread between sts. Knit this thread through the back so that it twists and slants the new st to the left.

Right-slanting increase (M1R): Insert point of left needle from back to front under thread between sts. Knit this thread through the front so that it twists and slants the new st to the right.

Make your own sample swatch:

With size 9 needles and worsted yarn, cast on 18 stitches. Work knit two, purl two ribbing for three rows. Change to Stockinette stitch and continue for two rows. On next right side row, work M1R or M1L increases in full fashion as follows:

Row 1 (RS): K2, M1R, knit to last 2 sts, M1L, K2.

Row 2: Purl.

Row 3: Knit.

Row 4: Purl.

Work rows 1–4 another 3 times.

On next RS row, shape armhole. Bind off 4 sts at beg of next 2 rows. On next RS row, shape armholes by working full-fashion dec as follows:

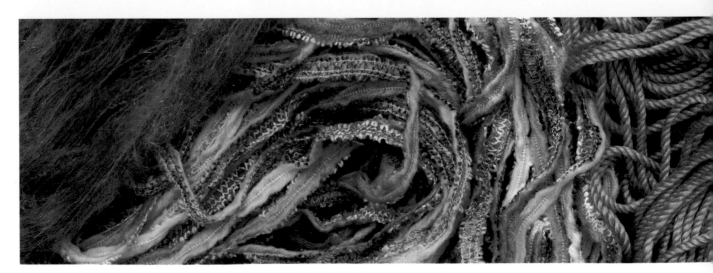

Row 1: K2, ssk, knit to last 4 sts, K2tog, K2.

Row 2: Purl.

Work rows 1 and 2 another 4 times.

Change all sts to K2, P2 ribbing and work for 3 rows. BO in pattern.

To keep the ssk neat, work on the tips of your needles.

Take a look at the swatch and see how each increase and decrease becomes part of the design and leans in the correct direction. Always think about the direction that you want the stitches to move and use the appropriate instruction.

If you prefer to work a traditional bar increase (knit in the front and knit in the back of the same stitch), place this increase on the second stitch at the beginning of the row and on the third stitch from the end of the row.

Shaping can also be moved away from the side edges to the interior of a piece, much as vertical darts are placed in sewing. This provides a more natural taper and is especially desirable for large amounts of taper such as that found in swing coats, where the bottom edge will have a better shape. Large numbers of decreases along a side edge make a flat-bottomed triangle (below left) whose sides can droop, while decreases placed in the interior form a more natural curved hem (below right).

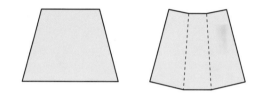

In some cases design elements inside the knit piece allow you to move the shaping to each side of these elements, leaving the edges completely unchanged. This helps the design sit on the body properly, following your natural curves (we aren't paper dolls, after all!). Pattern stitches or color work may require that shaping remain along the side edge. Be sure to work a swatch in your pattern stitch and experiment with increases and decreases to see how easily the pattern can be adjusted.

Body and Neckline Styles

✦ **Pullovers** are exactly that: there is no front opening and the garments are "pulled over" the head. Pullover neck shaping includes a shallow V-neck, three different rounded shapes, and a boatneck. The rounded shapes are scoop, which is low and appropriate for tank-top styles; crew neck, which is high and the basis for building traditional ribbed neckbands, turtlenecks, and mock necks; and jewel, which is in between and usually finished simply. Boatnecks are straight across with no shaping and are wider than shaped necklines. Funnel necks are built onto boatneck shaping.

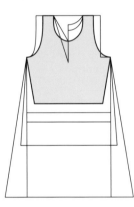

Cropped length with taper
Sleeveless cut-in armhole
Scoop neck

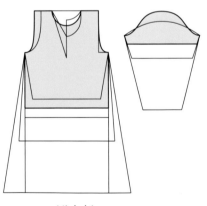

High-hip no taper
Set-in cap sleeve
Jewel neck

✦ **Classic cardigans** are pullovers split up the middle, with an overlapping button band, and are often worked with no taper but more ease. Deep V, shallow V, and crew necklines all work well for classic cardigans. Shawl collars are built upon deep V-necks and turned collars are built upon crew shaping. Ribbed, garter, or crocheted bands can finish any of the three.

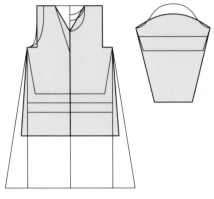

Fingertip jacket with taper
Shallow V-neck
Modified-drop long sleeve

✦ **Tailored jackets** are also pullovers split up the middle, but they have a center front that just meets, and so are appropriate for dressier styles with button-and-loop, zipper, or no closure. Deep V, shallow V, or crew necklines work here. Simple edges such as crochet, reverse crochet, and applied I-cord are best. Because there may not be a closure, more ease should be allowed so the jacket doesn't gap in the front, or tapering should be used.

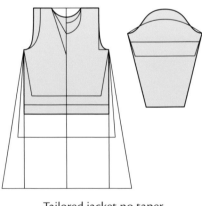

Tailored jacket no taper
Set-in sleeve cap
Crew neck

◆ **Coats** are oversized cardigans: longer and with taper built in or generous in circumference if straight. There is overlap for the front closure and extra ease should be considered to accommodate other garments underneath and also for narrowing that occurs as the fabric's weight draws down. Deep V, shallow V, and crew necklines work well with this style.

Set-in armhole shaping
True sleeve cap

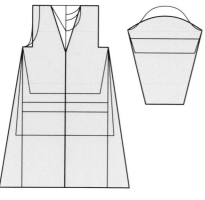

Long coat with taper
Modified-drop long sleeve
Deep V-neck

Modified-drop sleeve
Gently rounded sleeve cap

Sleeve and Armhole Styles

◆ **Sleeveless** styles can have either standard or cut-in armholes. Standard armholes will hit shoulders just inside where the arm joins the shoulder and allow for a bit more coverage. Cut-in armholes are another inch or so inside of the shoulder line.

◆ **Cap, short, and long sleeves** can be attached to either standard set-in armhole shaping, where the armhole is rounded and the top has a true cap, or to a modified drop shaping, where the armhole cuts in sharply once, and then works straight up. Modified drop sleeves have a gently rounded cap, with a shoulder that extends beyond the natural shoulder line.

FAQ   **My set-in sleeves never seem to fit right. Any hints?**

The entire fit of a sweater flows from the shoulders down. Tailored, fitted sleeve caps impart a neat appearance to the whole garment. A set-in sleeve cap that droops down the arm looks ill fitting and adds visual weight to heavier sizes while making small sizes seem to swim in big brother's hand-me-downs. A proper-fitting set-in sleeve must have a shoulder width that is just inside the top of the arm. Since the shoulders carry a sweater's entire weight, special attention should be paid to ensure that front and back pieces are tightly joined and that the seam will hold its width. Many people choose to knit shoulder seams together with a three-needle bind off, and while this technique certainly works and is visually attractive, it is not something that we recommend. The combined weight of all pieces can stretch the seam, often causing sleeves to become too long and the sleeve cap attachment to sag down the arm. Additionally, weight is placed on live stitches, and if one strand breaks the shoulders will part and knitting will run just like a nylon stocking. We recommend binding off all shoulder edges firmly (to the actual desired shoulder width measurement with no give), and then joining them together firmly, either with invisible seaming or by working Kitchener stitch (usually used to graft live stitches) over the bound-off edges to mimic the knitted portion, or by holding the right sides together and slip stitching through both pieces with a crochet hook. The most important aspect is to make sure the initial shoulder width is correct and to alter the body pieces if it is not.

Shoulder width too wide, allowing set-in sleeves to droop below top of armhole

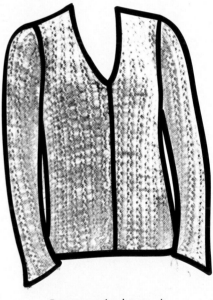

Proper set-in sleeves sit just inside top of arm.

Step 3: What Size Am I?

The chapter "With You in Mind: Custom-Fitting Techniques" (page 22) takes you step by step through custom measurements. No true universal sizing exists: Laura, who at 5' 3" has broad shoulders, a short torso, and an athletic build, wears sizes that range from an 8 to a 12 in ready-to-wear and uses a size 14 sewing pattern. She makes a finished bust that ranges anywhere from 36" for a dressy sweater or summer top to 44" for a coat or jacket. This lack of continuity is why we decided to eliminate size designations and use only inch measurements to distinguish one size from another. So, from this day forth, you are no longer a size!

It's important to know all of the nuances of your own shape for truly great-fitting garments, so take time to fill in the measurement chart. Once you have selected a garment style and yarn, the next step is to determine the amount of ease you desire. Consider the following:

✦ **Is the garment short or long?** The longer the garment, the more ease required.

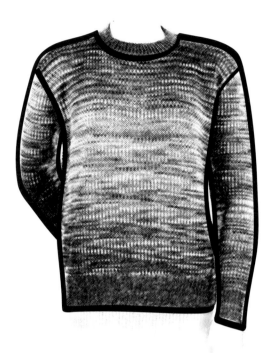

Longer garments require enough ease to fit over the hips.

✦ **Is the garment a cardigan or pullover?** Cardigans need to have enough ease to allow for garments worn under them; pullovers may be more fitted if dressier, or larger if they're sporty or if a turtleneck will be worn underneath.

Shorter garments require less ease.

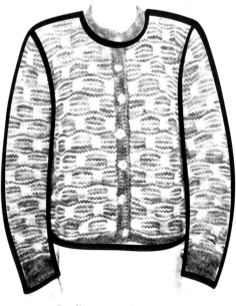

Cardigans require more ease than pullovers.

15

Pullovers require less ease.

◆ **What is the yarn like — thick or thin, soft or stiff?**
Thick or stiff yarns should have enough ease for
comfort of wear, but not so much that they take
on a size of their own and make one seem larger.
Soft or thin yarns can either be fitted or have a lot
of ease for a draped look. Look at ready-to-wear:
loose and flowing garments are made of very thin,
soft material, while thicker wools tend to be tailored for a close fit.

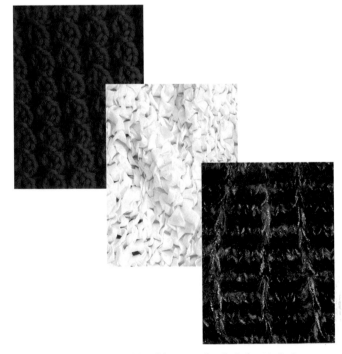

Firm yarn; drapable ribbon; and soft, lofty Mohair

◆ **Is there a large difference between your bust and
hip?** Be sure to make the size that accommodates
the larger measurement; if the difference is sub-
stantial (more than 4"), consider adding taper in
either direction, regardless of the style.

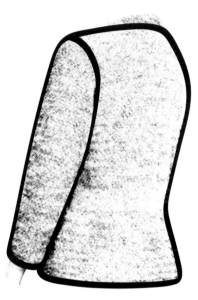

Taper can be added to accommodate a significant
measurement difference between bust and hips.

◆ **Are your shoulders square or sloped?** If square,
you may choose to finish your shoulders straight
across in one bind off. If sloped, select the shaped
shoulder option (page 35).

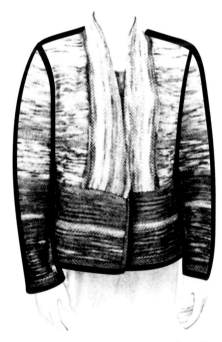

Sloping the shoulders gives a more fitted look.

FAQ

My shoulder width is narrower than your measurements. If everything flows from the shoulders, how do I make that adjustment?

The "Finished Measurement Chart" on page 26 gives measurements upon which the templates are based. Find the difference between *your* measurement and the chart measurement for your size, and then multiply that difference by the gauge. The result is the number of stitches that must be added to the template decreases during armhole shaping to achieve the correct size. Simply continue decreasing until the extra stitches have been removed.

For example, you are making a 42" sweater with set-in sleeves at four stitches per inch. Shoulder width for that size and style is 14½", but you want shoulders of 13". The difference (1½") multiplied by gauge (four) equals six stitches, or three additional stitches to be decreased per side. These can simply be added to the end of the specified decreases, in the work-even portion above these decreases, which leaves the armhole the same depth but narrows the shoulder. If there are many more decreases to be made, move some of them to every other row. Conversely, if the shoulders need to be wider, the same formula will tell how many fewer stitches to decrease. If there is a very great difference in shoulder width between you and the template, you may consider tapering the body along the side seam to remove some excess fabric before armhole shaping begins. We sized the templates with women in mind, so if you choose to make a man's sweater it is likely the shoulder width will need to be increased.

Notice that our charts do not refer to a size as "Small," "Medium," or "Large," but simply as a finished bust/chest measurement. Select the size you will make from the desired finished measurement of the garment once you have taken into account all of the preceding factors.

Customize your size by referring to the measurements taken in the chapter on fit. The most crucial difference between people's sizes, and the most important fitting point, is the shoulder-width measurement. Everything about the way a garment fits flows from how it sits on the shoulders. Thin people can have broad shoulders; large people can have narrow shoulders. Our sizes have been written progressively larger: as girth increases, so do length, shoulder width, and armhole depth. The increases are proportional, but notice that although girth numbers change dramatically, measurements such as shoulders change far less. So, if you are making a large size, there will be many more decreases for armhole shaping to get to an appropriate shoulder measurement than if you were making a small size. Likewise, if you are making a small size, there may be very little shaping. Check the armhole depth and make note of any change you wish there. If the armhole depth changes, the sleeve width at the top (for a modified drop) or the cap depth (for a set-in sleeve) will also change. For any change you need to make, locate the correct measurement on the size chart, and then refer to the stitch numbers on the template pages for that size.

From small to large—the templates cover it all!

FAQ **Does my body size alter the amount of ease I need?**

We can spend days talking about ease in a garment. When you look at a template size, it's indeed just that—the finished circumference measurement of the garment. The amount of preferred ease will vary from person to person. It's a good idea to go through your own closet and select some favorite garments in different styles, such as a shell, cardigan, and jacket. Make a copy of the actual body measurement form and measure each finished garment, noting the specific garment at the top for future reference. In a way, you are creating a set of template measurements that are now your own personal preferences. Compare the difference in these finished measurements against your body measurements and you can see how much ease you like for each different garment style. Keep in mind that we all live in different climates, with some of us having multiple seasons while others have only one or two. Some enjoy more closely fitted garments and others prefer them loose. This simple comparison may change your ideas of how much ease you think you like. In addition, finer fabrics with drape often require more ease since they flow down the body, while stiffer fabrics suitable for coats and jackets look better if they are tailored to fit. Excess ease in stiff or thick fabrics simply makes the wearer look larger as the garment takes on a shape of its own.

Steps 4–7: Pattern Writing

Turn to the "Finished Measurement Chart" on page 26 and find the column for your finished size. Copy the measurements onto the style diagram (page 30) so you have a ready reference as you knit.

Your blank pattern worksheet should already have gauge and needle size entered at the top. Turn to the pages for your gauge and select the column with your finished bust/chest measurement. Following the instructions at the left side for the body style you have

selected, enter the numbers from the column for your size onto the blank pattern. The blank spaces and the size charts are labeled with letters that correspond to the numbers you need to find.

If you are adding a pattern stitch, adjust the pattern numbers as follows:

1. Subtract the number of edge stitches from the cast-on total. The repeat of a pattern stitch is written as "multiple of ___ sts plus ___ st(s)." The edge stitches are the "plus" number.

2. Divide the remaining stitches by the multiple. If the divisor is even, you are all set. If it is a fraction, you need to round up or down to make it even. Round up if you wish a bit more ease (or if the fraction is over .5). Round down if there is plenty of ease (or if the fraction is under .5).

For example, the suggested cast on for a 40" circumference (a 20" back) is 90 stitches for a gauge of 4.5 sts = 1". The pattern repeat is 6 plus 3. Subtract 3 from 90 = 87. Divide 87 by 6 = 14.5 repeats. Round up to 15 repeats times 6 = 90 stitches plus 3 = 93 stitches cast on.

There are several things you can tweak for perfect results. We did not allow for selvage stitches. If your garment is close fitting, add two stitches to every piece for seaming. The rate of increases and decreases for taper and V-neck shaping are based on the stated body length with set-in armhole shaping. Cut-in (sleeveless) and modified-drop armholes change the garment length to the armhole by a small amount, but the rates of increase and decrease will hold true. If your row gauge is different from the stated row gauge, find a row gauge that matches yours from a different chart. Use the stitch numbers from the matching stitch gauge, but find a column (regardless of the size) whose number of increases or decreases is the same as yours in the chart with the matching row gauge. Whatever the rate of change is in that column, use that number (decrease one stitch each edge every ___ row) as your rate.

Cast-on numbers are written for a borderless finish (no ribbing). Many styles begin with simple rows of garter stitch (which require no change in numbers) or are in fabric flat enough that a crocheted edge is all that is necessary. A good rule of thumb for any ribbing or garter stitch on a border is to use needles two sizes smaller than the body. Additionally, ribbing stitches should be about 10 percent fewer in number than body stitches. Make notes of any changes between border stitches and body/sleeve stitches.

Contrary to our early knitting teaching, row gauge is not something to be ignored, but a helpful tool both in ensuring good results and in planning quantities of yarn. If your row gauge varies much from the stated gauge on a pattern, you will use more yarn (if you knit more rows per inch) or less yarn (if you knit fewer rows per inch) than the pattern calls for. We have found over the years that variations in row gauge are the biggest differences from one knitter to another. Needle sizes can be changed to match a stitch gauge—but the row gauge still might not match. Not to worry; most of the time this only impacts yarn quantity, because knitting that is worked from the bottom is knit to a measurement. Fashion yarns in particular, because they might be heavy or highly textured, tend to have fewer rows per inch. Many pattern stitches, especially those with slipped stitches, have more rows per inch. Be aware of differences, and make adjustments as needed. See page 40 for additional discussion on row and stitch gauge.

Ribbed and cabled stitches require some extra planning. Because these stitches tend to pull in, the ratio of stitches to rows changes, with more stitches in relation to rows per inch. This mostly affects sleeve cap and shoulder shaping, where the extra stitches will result in cap shaping that occurs too slowly, leaving a large number of stitches at the top or a too-wide shoulder seam. The answer is to increase the rate of cap decreases; for example, a ribbed sweater might have decreases that occur every row instead of every other row. When binding off at the top edge, decrease stitches as you bind off by working two stitches together as many times as necessary to return to a normal number of stitches (compare the yarn's gauge in stockinette stitch to the gauge in pattern—the stockinette numbers are a more normal gauge). A ribbing pattern with more knits than purls will not need as many decreases as a regular ribbing. Cables can be decreased in the middle of the cable, usually by two stitches.

Two ribbed swatches: one relaxed, one slightly stretched. Take care when measuring your gauge.

The Fudge Factor

Every designer employs a fudge factor, and we are no exception. Size proportions and incremental changes in this book are based on our joint years of designing, teaching, measuring, and "fixing." When writing different sizes and calculating numbers of stitches, fractions invariably show up. In almost every instance, we rounded up, unless the fraction was ¼" or less.

Additionally, finer gauges allow more precise shaping; conversely, larger gauges require more fudging. In smaller gauges, you will find that there are distinct differences between sizes; as gauges get larger, the numbers will tend to stay the same for several sizes before changing.

How Much Yarn Do I Want?

Of course, we all want as much yarn as we can afford! However, since few of us have unlimited yarn budgets, we want a realistic idea of how much yarn to buy for a given garment. This is one of the toughest areas to address, since so many factors influence final yarn requirement. The "Yardage Chart" (page 21) shows suggested yardages for each range of gauges in each range of sizes. We have organized it this way to give you guidance, but there is no ultimate answer. Important questions to ask when deciding on quantities:

✦ **Am I a tight or loose knitter?** Generally, even when knitting a stitch gauge, a loose knitter will knit a looser row gauge (that is, fewer rows per inch) than a tight knitter (more rows per inch). Tighter knitters will need more yardage.

✦ **Is my garment on the smaller or larger side of the size range?** Obviously, slightly smaller garments will require less yardage; larger sizes, more.

✦ **Is the gauge on the smaller or larger side?** In this case, the smaller gauge needs more yardage (more stitches and rows per inch, thus more yardage needed); the larger gauges, less.

✦ **Is there a pattern stitch?** Pattern knitting usually uses about 25% more yarn. This is especially true when more than one color is used. The extra goes to carrying yarn along the back and to the remnants of skeins left when all knitting is complete. Cables and other stitches that pull in can be compensated for by using the chart for the smaller gauge range (taken over the cables or ribbing), but remember that although the stitch gauge got smaller, the row gauge did not and you can compromise between the yardage requirements.

Whatever you calculate your needs to be, buy an extra skein. When the first piece is completed, check to see how much yarn has been used. Hopefully you are on target, but if you think you might be close, now is the time to get another skein, before the yarn, color, or dye lot is changed or discontinued. As much as we value our hard-earned dollars, the real heartbreak is in investing a lot of money and time into a project that cannot be finished! Any extra yarn can go into your stash for use with other yarns later and can be invaluable if you need to repair something in the future.

FAQ

I always seem to run out of yarn. Any suggestions?

Yarn is a funny thing. Any particular yarn style is manufactured for only so long. Dye lots are only so big. Knitting styles and folklore have us do different things. All of this makes it hard to pin down exactly how much yarn will be needed and makes it difficult to obtain more at a later date. It's always best to buy an extra skein of each yarn while the dye lot is available. Doesn't everyone have a yarn stash? If you're anything like us, we're sure you have lots of wonderful yarn waiting to be knit. Having an extra skein will give you some leeway and any remaining yarn will go into stash, which can then percolate like starter for sourdough bread. Often yarn is purchased based on an existing pattern without examining all of the details or making a swatch. Make sure your size template is completed, compare it to the size of the pattern, and adjust accordingly. And, by all means, check your row gauge. Often knitters who repeatedly run out of yarn are knitting tighter than specified row gauges. Of course they are going to need more yarn—they need more rows to get to the same measurement!

If you have concerns about yarn quantity, knit multiple pieces at the same time. If you run low and must add another yarn, adjust the size, or shape things differently to finish the sweater, the pieces will match if they are worked concurrently. Strive for a design solution that will look as if it was purposeful and not a panicked "fix." Try to join new yarn at the end of a row so that tails have a seam in which to be buried. If yarn quantity is an issue, join where you can, making sure joining knots are tight and tails are long enough to bury.

Yardage Chart

The following chart indicates approximate total yards of yarn required for the various styles and sizes. Use these amounts as guidelines only. Actual amounts will vary depending on type of yarn, pattern stitch, and individual differences in tension of knitting.

Style/Sizes	6 sts = 1"	5–5.5 sts = 1"	4–4.5 sts = 1"	3–3.5 sts = 1"	2–2.5 sts = 1"
Sleeveless	Yards	Yards	Yards	Yards	Yards
30"–36"	600–700	500–700	450–600	350–450	200–300
38"–44"	850–1000	750–950	650–850	500–650	300–400
46"–52"	1000–1150	1050–1250	900–1050	700–850	500–600
54"–60"	1200–1350	1300–1450	1100–1250	900–1000	600–700
Short Sleeves					
30"–36"	1000–1150	950–1050	800–900	750–850	350–450
38"–44"	1200–1350	1150–1350	1000–1150	875–1000	450–550
46"–52"	1400–1550	1350–1500	1200–1350	1000–1125	550–650
54"–60"	1600–1800	1550–1700	1400–1600	1150–1300	650–750
Long Sleeves					
30"–36"	1300–1600	1050–1300	900–1200	600–900	600–700
38"–44"	1750–2100	1350–1600	1300–1600	950–1200	700–800
46"–52"	2300–2500	1650–1800	1650–1950	1250–1500	850–1000
54"–60"	2650–2800	1850–2200	2000–2200	1550–1700	1050–1200
Fingertip Jacket					
30"–36"	1600–1750	1450–1550	1250–1350	900–1100	700–800
38"–44"	1800–1950	1600–1750	1450–1550	1150–1350	800–900
46"–52"	2000–2150	1800–1950	1600–1750	1400–1550	900–1000
54"–60"	2200–2350	2000–2150	1800–1950	1600–1750	1000–1100
Long Coat					
30"–36"	2100–2800	1850–2650	1600–2300	1200–1700	900–1000
38"–44"	3000–3500	2800–3350	2450–2850	1750–2100	1000–1100
46"–52"	3600–4050	3500–3950	2950–3350	2150–2500	1150–1250
54"–60"	4100–4500	4000–4250	3400–3600	2550–2700	1300–1400

WITH YOU IN MIND

Custom-Fitting Techniques

Before starting your next knitting project, ask yourself: do I know the size I need to make for the finished sweater to fit the way I want? This section takes you through the process of answering this question in detail. Our goal is to help you feel more comfortable about selecting the right size for yourself or the lucky recipient of your talents.

Body Measurements

When we teach classes on fit and style, everyone cringes when we talk about taking body measurements. Then, when we get down to it, laughter takes over and the reality is that we learn more about ourselves and what we need to create a sweater that truly fits. Grab a tape measure (a new, nonretractable one is preferable) and a friend. Make a photocopy of the blank "Actual Body Measurement Chart" (page 25) and you're ready to start.

Accurate body measurements are important for deciding which size you will follow in a preprinted knitting pattern and which numbers to use when custom designing your own garment. You'll learn how to take fitted body measurements and how much ease to add for the different design styles. Then you can find the proper size on the appropriate gauge template.

Working with a friend is a good idea, since taking your own measurements is not easy. If you do decide to work alone, please do so in front of a long mirror, standing tall and always looking forward. This will ensure that the area you are measuring is correct and that the tape measure is in the right place and is completely straight. If you work with a friend, measure your friend and let your friend measure you. Follow the "Actual Body Measurement Chart" as you go. The process of measuring is the same for a woman, man, or child. An alternative to measuring the body is to measure a finished sweater. While this is not as accurate, it will work if you take the same measurements and fill in the chart. If you do measure a finished sweater, note on the chart that these measurements are not "fit" measurements, but finished measurements, including ease.

1A. **Bust/Chest.** Measure around the body at the fullest part of bust/chest. Be sure that the tape fits, but is not digging in, and follows an even horizontal line around body.

1B. **Back.** Measure from center of underarm on one side to center of underarm on the other side across back only.

2. **Waist.** Measure completely straight around narrowest part of body between bust and hip. This is usually just inside waistband of pants or a skirt. Again, tape should fit but not dig in. You may not have a waist that is narrower than your bust or hip, but this measurement is still useful and will help ensure that accurate taper is used for longer pullovers, jackets, or coats and for cropped tops.

3. **Hip/Bottom.** Measure around fullest part of hip and bottom. It is important to be honest about where you are measuring, since some of us have generous tummies, some of us have prominent bottoms, and some have both. Be sure to write down the larger number. When making a coat of any style or a longer classic cardigan, this measurement will make a difference in taper, fit, and ease.

4. **Sleeve Length.** Measure from top of shoulder down to desired length for a short sleeve (A) garment and down to wrist, running the tape measure along the arm, for a long sleeve (B) garment. Note that this measurement is for total length and includes both sleeve length to underarm and sleeve cap.

5. **Back Neck Width.** This is never easy to take and is truly a visual measurement. I usually have the person I am measuring stand facing me. I hold the tape behind their head and measure in a straight line from ear to ear. The back neck controls the opening for the head to fit through. If too much is left open, the sleeves and body do not stay up, and if the opening is too small, the head will not fit through.

6. **Finished Length.** This measurement starts at the bone at the base of the back of the neck with the tape measure going straight down. A is the length for cropped tops, B is the length for high-hip pullovers/jackets, C is the length for low hip, D is the length for fingertip, and E is the length for coats. For each measurement be sure you are standing straight and not leaning in any direction, since leaning will change the length measured.

7. **Upper Arm.** For some reason, we get the loudest groans when we measure this in a class setting. Wrap tape measure around fullest part of upper arm. Be sure that the tape is straight and that it's not digging in. Since most people make short sleeves to cover this area, we will then have the upper arm measurement for a short-sleeve cuff.

8. **Wrist.** Now we get to everyone's favorite measurement. Measure in a straight line around the wrist just above wrist bone when your hand is held up.

9. **Shoulders.** This is one of the most important measurements for sleeveless sweaters and for styles with set-in sleeves. A correct measurement will put the sleeve cap at the top of the shoulder for set-in sleeves and will cover up bra straps for sleeveless tops. With the person you are measuring facing away from you, place tape measure along the inside of the skin fold where the arm attaches to the body and measure horizontally across the shoulder blades to the same point on the other side. Hold the tape and check to be sure this is the correct place. Ask yourself: will the bra straps be covered? Will sleeve caps sit at the top of the shoulder if the sleeve is attached at this point? Adjust the tape in or out, depending on how you answer the questions and in relation to what you want to cover up or show.

10. **Armhole Depth.** Place a knitting needle horizontally under your armpit so that the ends stick out at the front and back. Measure from the needle up along body to the top of shoulder.

11. **V Depth.** Put the tape measure at the edge of neckline, at the center of shoulder where the seam would be, and run it straight down to your desired depth for a pullover (A) and for a cardigan (B).

12. **Rounded Neck Depth.** Put the tape measure at the edge of neckline, at the center of shoulder as for the V, and run it straight down to your desired depth for a crew neck (A), jewel neck (B), or scoop neck (C).

Now that you have taken measurements, sit down and relax. No matter what the numbers say, it's important to know that no one will see them when you are wearing the perfect-fitting sweater. What will be admired is how wonderful you look and how the sweater accentuates the parts of your body that you want to show off. Remember, we don't wear our size labels on the outside.

FAQ I learned in class how to take body measurements using the charts. Can I make copies of the chart and do this with my friends?

By all means, make copies of the actual body measurement chart and use this as a sizing template for every garment you make. We laugh about this all the time. Most people shake when we tell them that we are doing a full set of body measurements. We are all self-critical about our measurements until we treat them as just numbers, use them with the templates, and have a garment that looks great and fits perfectly. Then everyone wants to take measurements. Since we have removed standard size labels and work instead with inches and desired ease, the stigma of a "size" is removed. Be sure to note if the measurements include ease or not, and record how much ease on each piece. You will find this incredibly helpful for designing future garments. It can be a lot of fun to get your knitting guild together or go to your local yarn store and have a measuring night. Measure a friend so the numbers stay private, laugh as your learn more about your friends than you ever wanted to know, and continue to make garments that you're proud to wear.

Actual Body Measurement Chart

For: _____   Date: _____

1A. Bust/Chest: _____

1B. Back: _____

2. Waist: _____

3. Hip/Bottom: _____

4. Sleeve Length

    A. Short sleeve: _____

    B. Long sleeve: _____

5. Back Neck Width: _____

6. Finished Length

    A. Cropped: _____

    B. High Hip: _____

    C. Low Hip: _____

D. Fingertip: _____

E. Coat: _____

7. Upper Arm: _____

8. Wrist: _____

9. Shoulders: _____

10. Armhole: _____

11. V Depth

    A. Pullover: _____

    B. Cardigan: _____

12. Rounded Neck Depth

    A. Crew: _____

    B. Jewel: _____

    C. Scoop: _____

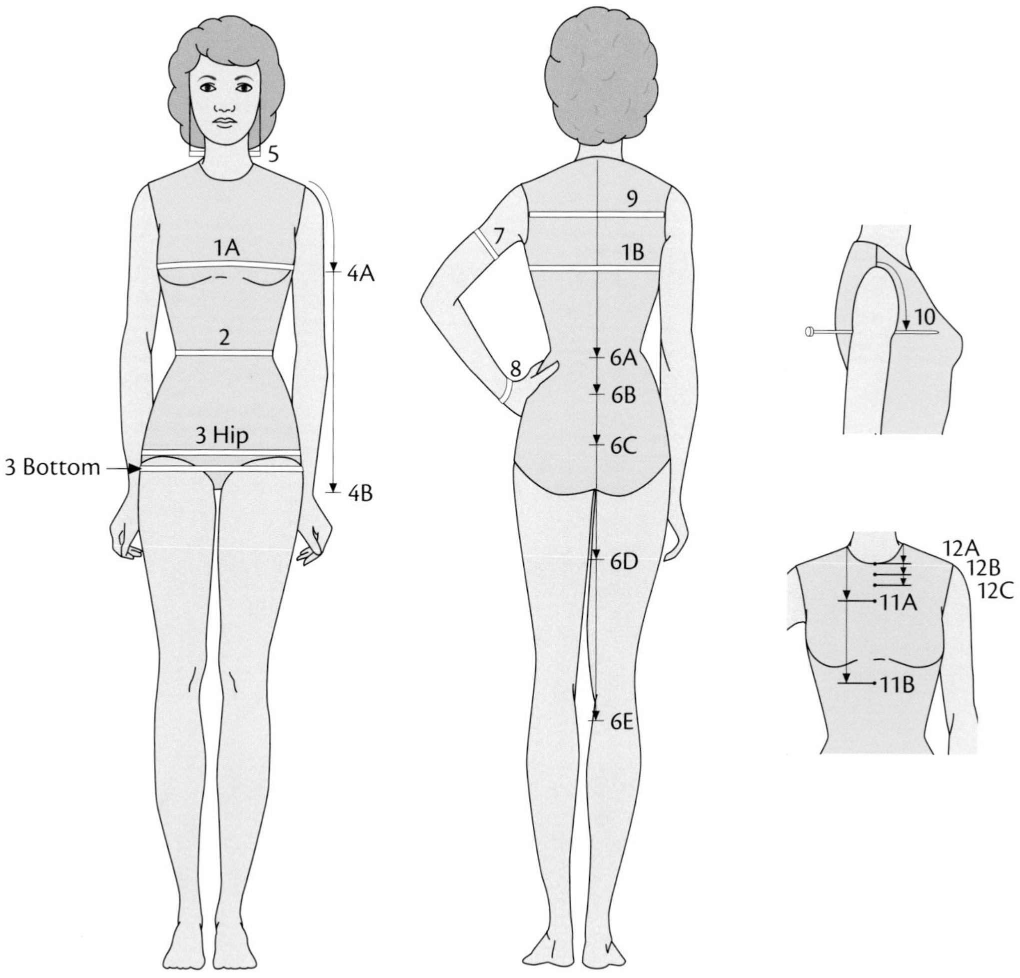

Finished Measurement Chart *(All measurements are in inches.)*

Refer to the "Style Diagram" on page 30 for identification of the letters mentioned below.

Finished Bust/Chest	30	32	34	36	38	40	42
Body Length (D+I)							
Cropped	18	18	18½	18½	19	19	19
High Hip	20	20	20½	20½	21	21	21
Low Hip	22	22	22½	22½	23	23	23
Fingertip	26	26	27	27	28	28	28
Long	38	38	39	39	40	40	40
Armhole Depth (I)							
Sleeveless	6½	6½	6½	7	7	7	7½
Set In	7	7	7	7½	7½	7½	8
Modified Drop	7½	7½	7½	8	8	8	8½
Neckline (from beginning of armhole)							
Crew	4½	4½	4½	5	5	5	5½
Jewel	3½	3½	3½	4	4	4	4½
Scoop or Shallow V	2½	2½	2½	2	2	2	2½
Deep V	-1	-1	-1	-1	-1	-1	-1
Shoulder Width							
Cut In	11	11	11½	11½	11½	12	12
Set In	12½	13	13½	13½	14	14	14½
Modified Drop	14	14	15	15	16	16	17
Back Neck Width							
Boatneck	8	8	8	8	9	9	9
All Others	5	5	5½	5½	6	6	6
Sleeve Length							
Set In							
Cap (to ua)	1½	1½	1½	1½	2	2	2
Cap (total L) 5½	5½	5½	6	6½	6½	7	7
Short Sleeve (to ua)	4	4	4	4	4½	4½	4½
Short Sleeve (total L)	8	8	8	8½	9	9	9½
Long Sleeve (to ua)	15	15	15½	15½	16	16	16
Long Sleeve (total L)	19	19	19½	20	20½	20½	21
Modified Drop							
Cap (total L)*	4½	4½	4½	5	5½	5½	6
Short Sleeve (total L)*	7	7	7	7½	8	8	8½
Long Sleeve (total L)*	18	18	18½	19	19½	19½	20

Measurement to underarm for cap, short, and long modified drop sleeve is total length minus 3".

44	46	48	50	52	54	56	58	60
19½	19½	20	20	20	20½	20½	21	21
21½	21½	22	22	22	22½	22½	23	23
23½	23½	24	24	24	24½	24½	25	25
29	29	30	30	30	31	31	32	32
41	41	42	43	43	44	45	45	46
7½	7½	8	8	8	8½	8½	8½	8½
8	8	8½	8½	8½	9	9	9½	9½
8½	8½	9	9	9	9½	9½	10	10
5½	5½	6	6	6	6½	6½	7	7
4½	4½	5	5	5	5½	5½	6	6
2½	2½	3	3	3	3½	3½	3½	3½
-1	-1	-1	-1	-1	-1	-1	-1	-1
12	12½	12½	13	13	13½	13½	14	14
15	15½	16	16½	17	17½	17½	18	18
17	18	19	20	20	21	21	22	22
9	9	9	10	10	10	10	10	10
6½	6½	6½	7	7	7	7	7	7
2	2	2½	2½	2½	2½	3	3	3
7	8	8	8	8½	9	9½	9½	
4½	4½	5	5	5	5	5½	5½	5½
9½	9½	10	10	10	10½	11	11½	11½
16½	16½	16½	17	17	17	17½	17½	18
21½	21½	22	22½	22½	23	23½	24	24½
6	6	6½	6½	6½	7	7½	7½	7½
8½	8½	8½	8½	8½	9	9½	9½	9½
8½	20½	20½	21	21	21½	22	22	22½

ua = underarm   L = length

Blank Pattern Worksheet

Refer to the "Style Diagram" on page 30 as you fill in
the numbers for the various components of your garment.

Style: _____

  Length: _____

  Optional taper: _____

  Sleeves:

    Length: _____

    Armhole style: _____

  Neckline style: _____

Finished bust/chest measurement: _____

Materials: _____

Needles: _____

Stitch Pattern (name): _____

  and (multiple) _____

Gauge: _____ sts and _____ rows = 1" (measured over 4" swatch)

Back

With size ____ needles, CO _____ sts (A, plus or minus any adjustments for border). Work desired border for ___".
Change needles, if necessary, and inc or dec _____ sts across next row. Total sts: _____ (A) (the number from
  the Finished Measurement Chart for your size).
Optional taper (cropped): Inc 1 st at each end every _____ rows _____ times (B). Total sts = _____ .
Optional taper (fingertip or long): Dec 1 st at each end every _____" _____ times (C). Total sts = _____ .
Work to _____" (D) (from diagram).

Shape Armhole

Cut-in or set-in: BO _____ sts at beg of next _____ rows (E). Dec 1 st at each end EOR _____ times (F).
  Dec 1 st at each end every 4th row _____ times (G). Total sts = _____ .
Modified drop: BO _____ sts at beg of next 2 rows (H).
Work even to armhole depth of _____" (I) (from diagram). **Total length of garment _____" (I + D)**
  (from diagram).

Optional Shoulder Shaping

BO _____ sts at beg of next _____ rows (determine this by following instructions on page 35) or BO all sts.

Front (Pullover)

Work as for back to _____" (desired length for chosen neck style—see Finished Measurement Chart). Cont to
  work armhole shaping as for back, and at same time . . .

Shape Neck

Boatneck: BO center _____ sts (J).
Any rounded style: BO center _____ sts (K). Attach yarn to 2nd shoulder, working both shoulders at once, BO _____ sts (L) at each neck edge once; BO _____ sts (M) at each neck edge once, dec 1 st at each neck edge EOR _____ times (N).

Any V style: Work to within 2 sts of center, dec 1 st by K2tog, attach 2nd ball of yarn and dec 1 st by ssk (division for V-neck made), cont to dec 1 st at each neck edge as established every _____ row _____ times (O).
When same length as back, shape shoulders as for back.

Front (Cardigan or Jacket)

Cast on _____ sts (P). Work border as for back, then change needles, if necessary, and inc or dec sts evenly across next row. (Determine as for back.)
Optional taper (fingertip or long): Dec 1 st at side edge only every _____ rows _____ times (Q).
Work to _____" (desired length to armhole shaping—see size charts and personal data).
Shape armhole as for back at side edge only. Work to desired length for chosen neck style (see Finished Measurement Chart).

Shape Neck

Any rounded style: BO _____ sts (R) at neck edge only, then BO _____ sts at neck edge only (L), BO _____ sts at neck edge only (M), dec 1 st at neck edge only EOR _____ times (N).

Boatneck: BO _____ sts at neck edge only (J).

Any V-neck: Dec 1 st at neck edge every _____ rows _____ times (O).
Shape shoulders as for back.

Sleeves

With size _____ needles, CO _____ sts (S). Work desired border, then change needles, if necessary, and inc or dec _____ sts across next row (depending on border—see back). Beg inc 1 st at each edge every _____ rows _____ times (T). When sleeve is desired length to underarm (see Finished Measurement Chart and personal data), shape cap.

Shape Cap

Set in: BO _____ sts (U) at beg of next 2 rows, dec 1 st at each edge EOR to cap depth of _____" (V).
BO all sts.

Modified drop: BO _____ sts at beg of next _____ rows (W). BO all sts.

Style Diagram

The letters identify the various components of the body styles that you'll need when reading the "Finished Measurement Chart" on page 26, to complete the "Blank Pattern Worksheet" on page 28, and to use as a reference with the "The Templates" beginning on page 59.

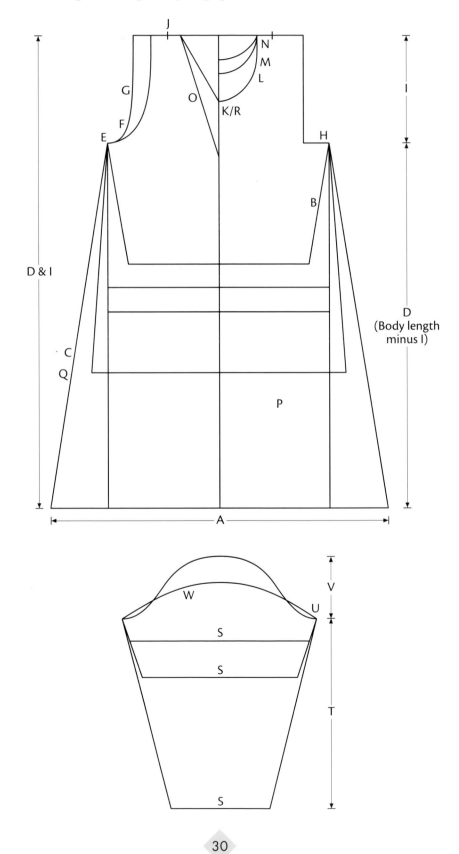

FAQ How do I adjust for a narrow back and full front, or if I carry most of my fullness in one area?

Here are the steps to think about. Initial body measurements give a chest/bust circumference. Preferred ease is added to arrive at a finished garment measurement. This new measurement is divided in half to become the width for front and back. In reality, most people (men included) have larger fronts than backs. If the front and back are more than a few inches different and we size by cutting the circumference in half, then the side seams won't be in place and the garment might not fit properly. Most of the time, the difference between front and back is not drastic, and the elasticity of knits allows for proper fit. In some cases, there is enough disparity to make an equally sized front and back ill fitting. If you find that your body is one that has big differences between front and back, you can easily follow two separate templates, one to make the back and one to make the front. Note the differences in the rate of increases or decreases along the body and watch the armhole shaping particularly. Any difference in stitch count between front and back must be equalized by the time shoulders are reached or they won't match when sewn. Take extra stitches off during armhole decreases. Any difference in armhole shaping will be absorbed during sleeve insertion.

Style Options

Let's move on to each of the style options and how to apply your measurements to them. As we look at different shapes, keep in mind the way you like things to fit. Always remember that we took "fitted" body measurements. You need to decide how much ease you want to add to the different styles. We make our recommendations, but the final decision is up to you.

Shell

This style is made to be worn under a suit jacket or on its own as a top. Most of the time a shell is sleeveless and more form fitting. Armhole shaping is very important and is often worked in full-fashion decreases so that the shaping becomes a part of the design. (A full-fashion decrease is a decorative detail done by placing decreases one or two stitches from the edges; see page 10.) Armhole shaping also begins higher and decreases at a slower rate for the best fit and most body coverage. Accurate shoulder measurements are very important here. The length of most shells is cropped or high hip so it will not peek out from the bottom of a suit jacket. If the shell is to be worn alone, the length can be made longer with straight shaping. We recommend adding either no ease or ease up to 2" to the largest measurement.

Shell—mid-hip length, cut-in armhole, jewel neck

Short-Sleeve Top

This style is similar to the shell but with a short sleeve of varying length, usually about 5" to the underarm. Some people like a modified short sleeve, or cap sleeve, with a sleeve length of 1" to 2". Armholes here come a bit lower, allowing for more ease because a short-sleeve top is rarely made to be worn under anything else. The body style is also easier, with less shaping, and you can decide the ultimate length you want. We consider the addition of about 2" ease to your bust measurement appropriate, depending on how you like your sweaters to fit and how thick the yarn is.

Short-sleeved top—low-hip length, set-in sleeves, crew neck

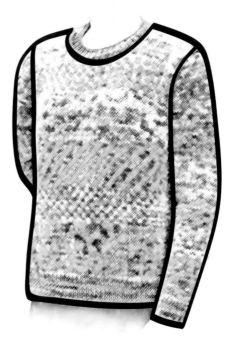

Pullover—low-hip length, set-in sleeve, jewel neck

Long-Sleeve Pullover

Laura describes this style as the perfect blank canvas on which to create, similar to the short-sleeved top but with a long sleeve. The body can be fitted with shaping, or you can add extra inches to the biggest body measurement and go long. For those with full figures, we often add 4" of ease to the largest measurement, go long in length, and leave a side-vent opening, allowing the sweater to move with the wearer. With no front bands to interfere visually, this style is great for color work and pattern stitches.

Classic or Updated Cardigan

Best described as "the sweater you always reach for" or "my favorite old friend," cardigans keep us warm and happy. Lengths vary from high hip to low hip and sometimes even longer. The length you select will guide the amount of ease needed. Compare the bust/chest measurement and the hip/bottom measurement. If you are making a true classic cardigan, it will have a straight body and enough ease so it doesn't hug against the largest portion of your body. We usually add 4" or more of ease to the largest measurement, always keeping in mind the stitch and yarn selection. Since this style is often casual, a modified-drop shoulder is a good choice, making the exact shoulder measurement less important and allowing ease to accommodate the garments underneath. Updated cardigans play with details such as front closures, collars, and pockets. No matter what you do, this style will remain faithful to you over the years.

Pullover—high-hip length, modified-drop shoulder, jewel neck

Tailored Jacket

Popularized by the House of Chanel, these elegant jackets mean business and will take you from casual to dressy. Straight in shape or with very subtle shaping, these jackets range from high or low hip to fingertip in length when worn. This style is often buttonless, so a blouse or knit shell can be worn underneath. Center fronts meet and don't overlap, so add enough ease to the bust measurement so the fronts don't gap.

Classic cardigan with moderate ease—
mid-hip length, set-in sleeve, crew neck

Updated cardigan with less ease: stick closure at bust allows lower portion to fall open—low-hip length, set-in sleeve, crew neck

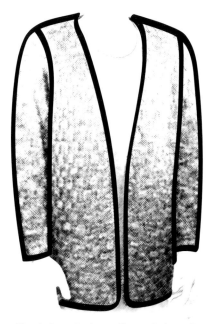

Classic long jacket—fingertip length,
set-in sleeve, deep V-neck

Tailored jacket—tapered hem to waist and back to bust, set-in sleeve, deep V-neck, sloped shoulder

Coat

This is where you can go crazy. Because coats are long and truly oversized, the options for textures, stitches, and needle-size variations are at your discretion. The important measurements here are shoulder, bust/chest, and hip/bottom. Most coats are A-line tapered to provide plenty of ease at the hip while staying narrower at the shoulder, or vertical and full for proper fit around the body, with at least 4" added to the hip measurement. Coats are often thicker than sweaters, worked from heavier yarns or multiple strands. This extra fiber weight affects the shape of garments, especially as they get longer, so allow extra width and always measure the length by holding the knitting up on the needle to allow for downward stretch. Remember that the width will narrow as the fabric weight pulls down. Additionally, armhole and neck shaping will elongate as well. A collar built onto a scoop neck might look as if it was built onto a shallow V (as in the illustration below), but a scoop neck is not really as deep as the V at the outset. A shallow V-neck would elongate even more. A modified-drop armhole is best because it allows you to wear clothing of any thickness underneath. This is a decorator's dream—have fun.

Long coat—long length, tapered to bust, modified-drop shoulder, no neck shaping

Oversized jacket—between low-hip and fingertip, tapered to bust, modified-drop shoulder, scoop neck

Other Factors to Consider

Since each of us was created different and our desires for fit range from "painted on" to "big and baggy," here are some things to think about before deciding which size to follow on the templates.

✦ *Where will I wear this sweater?* Dressy sweaters are often more fitted and casual sweaters more generous. Add more or less ease to your fitted body measurements to suit the end use.

✦ *What kind of yarn am I using and how will it hold up?* Play with your yarn(s) while making your stitch gauge. Try different needle sizes to get the suggested gauge. If you are starting from scratch and working from our templates, work with different needles until you appreciate the feel of the yarn and your stitch pattern is clear. Hang the swatch for a day and see if it grows. Wash or block your swatch carefully and see how the yarn changes.

✦ *What is my body style?* Am I full busted with a slender lower body, am I full bodied all over, or some other combination? You've taken your actual body measurements and you are no longer using "a size," so forget labels and make something that will actually fit. Stand in front of the mirror and look at how you like to wear your sweaters. Do you like things to fit tightly? If yes, add from 0" to 2" to your fit bust measurement. If no, add anywhere from 2" to 4". If your hips are bigger than your bust or if you have a tummy or bottom that sticks out, be sure to look carefully at your actual body measurements. Work a size that tapers to cover the fullness, or work a size that is large enough to go over the fullness and won't pull or stretch.

✦ *How do I like my sleeves?* Some of us want to show off our arms and some of us want to cover up excess flesh. Some of us have "hot flashes," and covering our arms adds heat to an already hot furnace. No matter what you decide, look at your actual body measurements and compare them to our Finished Measurement Chart. If necessary, make a sleeve for a different size and adjust shaping for the cap. Consider the type of sweater you want to make. Dressy sweaters call for set-in sleeves, while casual, easy sweaters work well with a modified-drop style. When you have wide stripes on a sleeve or a complicated stitch pattern that will cause problems with multiple-row bind offs along the cap, feel free to work a straight sleeve top with no shaping. The sleeve needs to be wide enough to fit into the armhole. Then, just bind off all stitches evenly across your last row.

✦ *How much neck do I like to show?* You've got that million-dollar necklace and you just have to show it off. You're knitting a sweater for that ski trip in Aspen. Both circumstances sound great and each one calls for a different style of neckline. Our template offers you many different variations. Think also about the type of collar finishing you want. For simple crochet edging, bring your neck

shaping up higher. If you want borders, edges, or collars, bring your shaping down a bit to allow for the extra knitting that will be done.

✦ *Do I need to do shoulder shaping?* Look in the mirror at the slope or angle of your shoulders. If your shoulders are relatively straight from your neck to your arms, then bind off straight across each piece. If your shoulders are sloped, bind off each piece in steps, working from the armhole side edge in toward the neckline. We suggest that you bind off incrementally over 1" to 2" of rows. Keep in mind that you may need to start neckline shaping proportionately higher.

✦ *What type of finishing am I comfortable with?* This is a truly important question. The more complicated you make your knitting, the more complicated the finishing may become. Many of us turn our finished pieces over to a professional finisher. Laura insists on doing all of her own finishing so that she has ultimate control over the final product. If you are comfortable with your own skills, jump in and get started. A good reference book for finishing techniques is Nancie M. Wiseman's book *The Knitter's Book of Finishing Techniques* (Martingale & Company, 2002).

We hope that our examples enhance your awareness of the freedom that you have. Your body is not a standard. Designers use a set of standard sizes and very few people fit every one of the criteria that we use for calculating patterns. Always check a pattern before starting to be sure that all of the individual piece sizes will work for you. Feel free to change things. Watch how making a change will affect the other pieces that need to match during finishing. Be responsible for your knitting and be in control of making things fit. We all want to make the size that we feel we "normally" would buy. Each magazine and designer uses a different set of sizes and numbers and each adds a different amount of ease to patterns. It's more important to know your body and how much ease you like for the style you are going to make, and then adjust the instructions to best fit your needs. Forget the size label—we don't wear tags on the outside of our sweaters. Make it fit and enjoy the compliments!

FAQ How do I add front bands to a cardigan? Mine always pull up or droop.

Front bands will be one of the last steps in completing your garment and you are fortunate to have a gauge already done: the band at the bottom of the sweater. Hold the back piece up sideways, so the border is in the same direction as it will sit on the front. Have a friend hold the piece up or pin the top edge to a pillowcase draped over a hanger; take a total measurement of the border from one edge to the other. This mimics how the garment will behave when the same border is worked onto the front. Divide the measurement by the number of border stitches and you have a border gauge (which probably won't match the garment gauge). Measure the sweater's front edge, multiply this measurement by the border gauge, and voilá! You now know the number of stitches to pick up along the front. The same can be done around the neck edge, with the garment lying flat and a flexible tape measure going around the curves. For a V-neck, measure to the beginning of the neck and place a marker, and then again along the neck to the shoulder, across the back neck, and repeat on the other side. Keep the number of stitches to each point separate to help in picking them up evenly and keeping them centered. You will need to increase stitches where the front band turns to make the V-neck, so plan increases at each neck marker.

Beginning with the left front, with right side facing you and the same needle size as the other borders, pick up as if to knit the required number of stitches evenly spaced along the band edge. Work in the border pattern to the desired width and bind off in pattern. Make sure that the bind off is neither too tight (band will pull up) nor too loose (band will waver and not lay flat). Measure the left band for buttonhole spacing, keeping in mind that if it is a crew neck you will also put a button in the neck band. Make the right side band, making buttonholes in the middle.

How do I add a collar to a template sweater?

Garment shape can be viewed as a setup for finishing details and this includes necklines. You must plan the needed foundation to achieve the desired finished result, and neckline shaping will be dictated by collar style. The templates contain instructions for the following necklines, which are the basis for the collar style noted.

✦ **Crew (high rounded neck):** tight turtlenecks or neck bands. Think ski sweater.

A ribbed collar built onto a crew neckline can be worn up or folded down.

✦ **Jewel (medium rounded neck):** looser, cowl-style turtlenecks or shirt-style pointed collar on jackets.

A simple collar folds back from a jeweled neck.

✦ **Scoop (low rounded neck):** crocheted or ruffled edging or low, portrait-style collars.

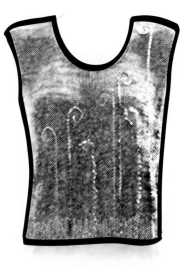

Scoop necks are perfect for tank styles and require little finishing.

✦ **Shallow V:** ruffle, thin ribbing or garter, crocheted edge, or crossed shallow shawl collar.

Partial ribbed band is worked along a shallow V-neck.

Simply finished garter-stitch bands are added after body is complete, and mitered slightly at the neck corners.

✦ **Deep V:** shawl collar, flounce, or ruffle.

A lush short-row flounce is
attached along a deep V neckline.

A narrow shawl collar and front band are added
after completion by picking up stitches.

✦ **Straight up with no shaping:** fold-back collarless lapels, suit-coat-style lapels when combined with a shirt-style collar, or funnel neckline (stand-up collar with no shaping).

Fronts worked straight up can
be turned back for lapels.

Collars can be added afterward or knit along with the fronts. Once again consider the idea that for every action there is a reaction. If I want a funnel neck, what do I have to change at the neck shaping? Where do I want a folded collar to fall, and where do I place the neckline to get it right? In most cases, you won't have to change neck shaping as outlined in the templates. It is simply a matter of deciding on the specific collar shape and building it onto the existing body pieces. Here are a few guidelines:

✦ A fold-over collar should be built onto a sturdy, tightly knit base where it joins the garment neck so that the collar stands up. As a guideline, pick up the same number of stitches as the back neck, and pick up one stitch per stitch or row along the front curved edge, using a needle at least two sizes smaller than the body. Work an inch or two with this tighter gauge, and then move to a larger needle, allowing collar to blossom.

✦ Turtlenecks should be worked in ribbing stitches so that they have maximum elasticity—large enough to pass over the head, but firm enough to return to neck size. Cowls can be knit more loosely, with larger needles and more stitches so they fall away from the face and neck.

✦ Ruffled collars and edgings should always be built onto firm, bound-off edges and not live stitches, which tend to spread, allowing the ruffled edge to look sloppy rather than ruffled. A row of slip stitches can be worked with a crochet hook along a too-loose edge to stabilize it before picking up stitches for a ruffle. Initially, pick up one stitch per stitch or row, and then increase in every stitch once for a slight ruffle, or in every stitch again for a really opulent, full ruffle. Binding off after just a few rows produces a pert, standing ruffle; working for several inches results in a more generous flounce. Increases can be made with yarnovers for ease of knitting.

✦ Shawl collars can be narrow or wide and can have stitches either in the same direction as the body or sideways. An integrated shawl collar can be worked by changing the stitch pattern at the center front and neck (from Stockinette stitch to ribbing, for example) and moving it over at the same rate as the template decrease shaping (without actually decreasing the number of stitches). The collar gets wider as more stitches are worked in the collar pattern.

For example, here's how to make a narrow, ribbed shawl collar that tapers to nothing at the center front. On the right front, on the next right side row, work two stitches in ribbing, place marker, and ssk (neck shaping begun). On following rows, work ssk decrease after the marker at the rate specified for the type of V neckline and gauge selected (you are decreasing in the body section), and at the same time, increase one stitch before the marker every second, third, or fourth row (depending on how quickly you want the collar to get wider) until the collar is the desired width. Continue to decrease after the marker for the total number of decreases specified in your gauge template. Work to the same length as the back. Bind off the shoulders and continue working collar stitches to the middle of the back neck. Repeat for other side, and then graft the center stitches.

To make a sideways shawl collar, pick up stitches along a deep V-neck at the rate of two or three stitches per four rows; pick up one stitch per stitch at the back neck and repeat for the other side. Work these stitches in pattern (usually ribbing) to the desired width, and then bind off in pattern. Collars worked in this manner are fun to stripe if there are several colors in your garment.

✦ For all neck treatments, be certain that bound-off edges on high necklines are loose enough to go over the head without stretching unduly.

Take a trip through your closet and observe how shape becomes a foundation for different styles and finishing details on a variety of garments. A few hours spent leafing through pattern books at the fabric store can be instructive also. Sewing pattern pieces are shown in flat diagram form on pattern inserts, so you can get a good idea of how to build more complicated designs. In fact, sewing patterns make great life-sized diagrams against which you can measure your progress. Go on—even if you don't sew, it can't be that scary!

FEELINGS

Gauge and Hand

Selecting a yarn for a pattern is almost as difficult as deciding which chocolate to pick from the box. So many yarns and colors, and you must narrow the selection to one, all the while hoping you have made the right choice.

The first step is to create a swatch. The label on the yarn or the pattern you are following will give a suggested needle size and recommended gauge. With the suggested needle, cast on at least 4" worth of stitches, and keep in mind that you may be working in a stitch with a pattern multiple.

Machine Wash Delicate/ Dry Flat
Merino Mia
Fiber Content: 100% Merino Wool
Color: *Thunderclap*
Net Weight: 2 oz. Yardage: 190 yds
#3 Needle, Gauge 6 ½ sts = 1" #4 Needle, Gauge 6 sts = 1"
Dye Lot #K0905

For example, if the suggested gauge is 4.5 stitches = 1" on size 8 needles, cast on at least 18 stitches (4.5 x 4"), casting on more, if needed, to get to the right multiple plus edge stitches. Work in the pattern stitch for at least 2". Stop to feel the swatch and look at the stitches. Ask yourself: Are they too loose or too tight? Are they even? Are they too soft or too stiff, too limp or too thick? Make the necessary needle adjustments, up or down, to correct what you don't like; if the fabric is too loose, go down several needle sizes; if too tight, go up. If you are fine-tuning, change one needle size and continue until you have at least 3" of knitting that works. Bind off your swatch.

Measuring gauge swatch

Right or wrong, always keep your swatches and attach a note card to them with the following information:

- ✦ **Yarn name/manufacturing company:** Dune by Trendsetter Yarns
- ✦ **Grams/yards per ball:** 50g/90yds
- ✦ **Needle size:** 9
- ✦ **Stitch used:** Ridge st, corrugated ribbing, stockinette st
- ✦ **Gauge:** stitches x rows/inch (3.5 stitches x 6 rows = 1" in pattern measured over a 4" square)

By attaching a card to each of your swatches, you can go back and use them again. We have used 10-year-old swatches to create some of our new sweaters—you just never know.

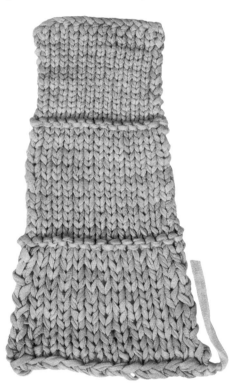

Swatches from top to bottom: too tight, just right, too loose

Determine the gauge by laying a tape measure or ruler on the swatch and dividing the number of stitches and rows by the inch measurement for each. If there is a fraction involved, round up to the nearest half stitch or row per inch.

Swatch notecard

FAQ   If I've done a stitch gauge, why does my knitting still not fit?

This question comes up repeatedly and for some of us is never answered. We have found that many knitters fall in love with a technique and the process of knitting, and then never stop and recheck the work once it is underway. Laura calls it "going on autopilot." You must always ask yourself:

✦ Am I relaxed while making my gauge swatch?

✦ Did my gauge change once I began?

✦ Did I do a large enough swatch?

✦ Do I like how the yarn feels on the needles or should I try another type or size of needle?

✦ Did I take an average gauge by measuring across my swatch or did I kind of guess at what I think the gauge is over an inch or two?

✦ Am I checking every piece as it flows from my needles, and once each is complete?

✦ Did I check the size I'm making to make sure it really is my size?

At the same time, if things have slipped out of control, stop for a moment and look at your knitting. Set it aside if you have an uncontrollable urge to rip! In most cases, things can be done to rescue the project. Don't give up until you try every possible fix. Be sure to check every piece along the way so that you catch a problem before it gets out of hand. Remember . . . knitters carry as much responsibility for a project's success as the designer. Knitting is teamwork.

I'm working an existing pattern and no matter how hard I try, I can't match both stitch and row gauge. Which is more important?

The biggest difference between knitters is row gauge. Different knitting styles produce different stitch-to-row ratios. There is no big gauge authority up in the cosmos dictating what stitch and row gauge each yarn should be, so be mindful at all times that a designer's gauge may not be your gauge. Different knitters can produce the same stitch gauge, and yet have a row gauge that varies up to a row per inch or more. So, my friend Susie gets 4 stitches and 6 rows while I get 4 stitches and 6½ rows per inch. Guess what? We are both knitting "to gauge," but I'll use more yarn than Susie will since it takes me one more row of knitting for each two inches of fabric!

Knitting is a formula: stitches per inch multiplied by the desired measurement. Our templates lay out the math for nine gauges and thirty sizes with myriad style options, and we had to assume a row gauge to determine armhole, neck, and sleeve shaping. For an existing pattern, the designer has done the same thing. Based on this, it is most important to match stitch gauge so the garment will fit widthwise. As a knitter in charge of your

project's success, you must really know your knitting for everything to work correctly.

Every knitter has a different knitting style and you may have to adjust your needle size up or down to match a suggested stitch gauge. With the templates, matching a gauge is less important than judging whether you like the feel of your swatch, since you can pick the template that is appropriate to your specific gauge. Refer to the chapter "Feelings: Gauge and Hand" (page 40) for more information.

Once stitch gauge is met or determined, check row gauge and look at the pattern to decide if shaping must be adjusted. Pay particular attention to necklines, armholes, and sleeves. In many cases, no changes need be made. In some cases you will have to adjust shaping to fit a new row gauge. The templates can be used to help adjust an existing pattern to fit the new row gauge, and you can also use them to assist with a row gauge that doesn't match a pattern's stated one. See "Finished Measurement Chart" (page 26) for more information.

As important as gauge is, the feel or "hand" of a yarn can make a big difference in the success of your knitting. One of Laura's favorite stories about her early knitting career was when as a teen, she purchased a spongy, plied bouclé from a weaving store. There was no label, so knowing that gauge was important, she kept making swatches until the gauge matched the pattern she wanted. The gauge matched all right, but the finished vest was so stiff and thick it stood up on its own! Our goal, as always, is not just to have pieces of a sweater that look good, but also to have a finished sweater that we love to wear.

FAQ There are lots of new fibers available. How do I know how they will behave?

There are many exciting fibers being used for knitting yarns. Every day someone is inventing something new. Many unusual fibers such as milk, banana, soy, bamboo, and shell are formed into an emulsion and extruded. When this happens, a filament is created that can be spun into a finished yarn on its own either through chaining or twisting and can also be blended with another fiber.

We always advise experimenting with a yarn before taking on a full garment. Begin by taking a length of yarn to test: hold onto both ends of a long strand and pull. Watch what happens. Does it stretch, and then bounce back when released? Does it twist back on itself in a loop when relaxed? This can indicate over spinning, which can lead to bias when knit. Does the yarn feel hard before knitting? Does it lack body? Knit a large swatch and bind off, or knit a scarf. Measure the swatch, and then hang it on a hanger for a few days. Measure the swatch again. Did the measurement change? Many of the new fibers are beautiful and lustrous but don't have the necessary characteristics to retain shape. We call this ingredient "memory" and it's present in almost all wool and nylon fibers, but less so in cotton, rayon, and many new fibers.

Consider the following when selecting and combining different yarns to enhance good qualities and mask undesirable ones:

✦ Traditional plied knitting wools are predictable in their behavior because of their construction, with individual plies twisted in the opposite direction from the finished twist. This cancels any pent-up energy that can lead to biasing and provides a nice elasticity that is pleasant to work on.

Plied yarns

✦ Often fashion yarns have an exciting look, but they can have drawbacks when knit into fabric. Bouclés can be limp. Rayon and silk stretch over time, and your stitches may appear too loose and uneven. Many fashion yarns have no elasticity—and thus no give on the needle—and tight knitters can find them difficult to work with.

Fashion and textured yarns

✦ Combining a difficult yarn with a well-behaved yarn can improve your knitting and make the experience better. Holding yarns together produces a thicker, overall patterned fabric.

Sparkly nylon, thin rayon component with squares of color, and thick spongy nylon yarns held together while knitting

✦ Striping with different yarns or using different types of yarns for colors A and B in a pattern stitch is another way to combine yarns and enhance good qualities while masking undesirable ones. A thinner knit fabric is created and the subtle stripes become a part of the design.

✦ If you have yarns with varied gauges and are working a slip-stitch pattern with two-row intervals, gauge differences of up to a half stitch per inch won't matter because one texture is laid over the other. The overall quality of the fabric evens out and compensates for individual gauge differences.

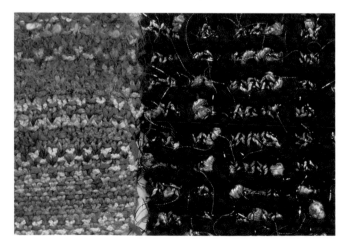

Slip-stitch pattern

Same yarns as above, worked in a stripe pattern

You have lots to think about and the knitting world is your oyster. With the knowledge you have at your hands, pick up some needles and create beauty.

CHANGING THE TONE

Ten Tricks for Custom Knits

Now that we have the basics down, let's play with ways to enhance the blank canvas that is our sweater. From simple tricks, such as stripes, to fancy cables and pattern work, these are the things we love about knitting—the endless possibilities that arise from two simple needles and a length of yarn. Refer to "Abbreviations and Glossary" on page 78 for a list of abbreviations.

Stripes

Three-color stripes are easy and fun to do. Cast on with A; then drop A and attach B. Work across with B; then drop B and attach C. Work across with C, and when you get to the end of the row—A is waiting for you! This is great for combining three yarns whose gauges may be different. Pick the needle that suits the middle-range yarn and the others will compensate. Try this with solids, with hand-dyed and multicolored yarn, and with contrasting textures. It's also a great way to showcase a special yarn—just combine it with more subdued yarns. The pattern can be simple stockinette or a more complicated textural stitch. To keep yarns from getting twisted as you work, place A to the left of you, B in front of you, and C to the right. Now, when you turn the work, hold it up and look what happens as the work is turned—one way twists, the other doesn't.

Ridge Stitch

(Multiple of 10 sts)

Row 1 (WS): *K5, P5; rep from *.

Row 2: Knit.

Row 3: *P5, K5; rep from *.

Row 4: Knit.

Rep rows 1–4.

Three different subtle textures in similar colors worked in ridge stitch.

One-row stripes in stockinette stitch: one solid, two multi-textured. Gold is switched with wine halfway through the swatch.

Half Linen Stitch

This stitch remains a favorite with us. Relatively simple to knit, it has the virtue of making the fabric a bit denser, which helps to tame many fashion yarns. If a yarn is too limp when knit in stockinette stitch, try the half linen stitch. Worked with multiple colors, either in two-row stripes or in one-row stripes using three colors (at left), it serves to blend and mix colors in an extremely pleasing way.

Half Linen Stitch

(Odd number of sts)

Row 1: *K1, sl 1 wyif; rep from *, end K1.

Row 2: Purl.

Row 3: K2, *sl 1 wyif, K1; rep from *, end K1.

Row 4: Purl.

Rep rows 1–4.

Two rows each of two similar multicolored yarns with different textures mix into an allover pattern.

Two rows each of solid and multicolored yarn; top half has the addition of a third yarn for one-row stripes.

Ribbing

Ribbing stitches add elasticity and produce form-fitting garments. Several variations include working some rows in garter stitch to give the look of ribbing without being clingy. Wide ribs can add quite a bit of texture and are easy to work, and using uneven numbers of knits and purls is a nice variation. Making ribbed garments in a much larger size will allow the ribbing to drape and flow.

K3, P3 Ribbing

(Multiple of 6 sts + 3 sts)

Row 1: *K3, P3; rep from *, end K3.

Row 2: P3, *K3, P3; rep from *.

Rep rows 1 and 2.

A wide ribbing mixes up the colors on one-row stripes of different colors and textures.

Mistake Ribbing

A wide ribbing that creates a waffle effect.

(Odd number of sts)

Row 1: K1, (P2, K2) across.

Row 2: P1, (K2, P2) across.

Rep rows 1 and 2.

A mistake ribbing is a narrow ribbing that is part seed stitch and thus might not be as elastic.

Lace Stitches

Stitches with yarn overs add a great deal of interest and are particularly suited to feminine, dressy garments. The openwork can soften a yarn, but really stiff yarns are better worked in another stitch. Lace stitches are particularly nice for mohair and other brushed yarns, where the core shows the stitches but the hair fills in some of the space.

Rickrack Faggoting Stitch

(Multiple of 3 sts + 1 st)

Row 1 (RS): K1, *YO, ssk, K1; rep from *.

Row 2: K1, *YO, P2tog, K1; rep from *.

Rep rows 1 and 2.

Ridged Ribbon Eyelet

(Odd number of sts)

Row 1 (RS): Knit.

Row 2: Purl.

Rows 3 and 4: Knit.

Row 5: *K2tog, YO; rep from *, end K1.

Row 6: Knit.

Pattern changes to allover lace:

Row 1 (RS): K1, *YO, K2tog; rep from *.

Row 2: Purl.

Row 3: K2, *YO, K2tog; rep from *, end K1.

Row 4: Purl.

Rep last 4 rows.

Kid mohair blended with a bumpy rayon is worked in an allover lace pattern.

Horizontal ridges and eyelets transform into allover lace.

Simple Slip Stitches

Slipping stitches is a great way to manipulate color. Because the colors both break up and mix together, this is a good choice for multicolored yarn. Slipping stitches causes the fabric to grow firmer, which can help with limp yarns.

Little Tent Stitch

(Multiple of 8 sts + 1 st)

Rows 1 and 3 (WS): K2, *P5, K3; rep from *, end P5, K2.

Row 2: K2, *sl 5 wyif, K3; rep from *, end sl 5 wyif, K2.

Row 4: K4, *insert needle under loose strand and knit next st, bringing st out under strand, K7; rep from *, end last rep with K4.

Rep rows 1–4.

Garter-Ridge Slip Stitch

(Multiple of 5 sts + 4 sts)

Row 1 (RS): *K4, sl 1 wyib; rep from *, end K4.

Row 2: *K4, P1; rep from *, end K4.

Rep rows 1 and 2.

Strong rows of slipped stitches give vertical emphasis to garter stitch.

Yarn carried across the front is picked up and knit in later for rows of diagonal lines.

50

Knit and Purl Stitches

Textural combinations provide a great deal of interest and are easy to work. Unlike ribbing stitches, which are knits and purls stacked up on one another, these patterns basically use purl stitches on a ground of knit stitches (or vice versa) to create texture.

Boxed Seed Stitch

(Multiple of 10 sts)

Rows 1, 3, and 5: *P1, K1, P1, K1, P1, K5; rep from *.

Rows 2, 4, and 6: *P5, P1, K1, P1, K1, P1; rep from *.

Rows 7, 9, and 11: *K5, P1, K1, P1, K1, P1; rep from *.

Rows 8, 10, and 12: *P1, K1, P1, K1, P1, K5; rep from *.

Rep rows 1–12.

Seed stitch provides a checkerboard pattern.

Textured Checks

(Multiple of 4 sts + 2 sts)

Row 1: Purl.

Row 2: Knit.

Row 3: *K2, P2; rep from *, end K2.

Row 4: P2, *K2, P2; rep from *.

Rep rows 1–4.

Textured checks look good on either side
(swatch changes halfway through).

Cables

Simple or complex, cables can add just the right dash to your knitting recipe. Whether as an allover pattern or a big accent running up a front or sleeves, cables provide deep textural interest. From something as simple as mock cables to elaborate braided strands, think cables!

Eyelet Cable

(Multiple of 5 sts + 2 sts)

Row 1 (RS): *P2, K3; rep from *, end P2.

Row 2: *K2, P3; rep from *, end K2.

Row 3: *P2, sl 1-K2-psso; rep from *, end P2.

Row 4: *K2, P1, YO, P1; rep from *, end K2.

Rep rows 1–4.

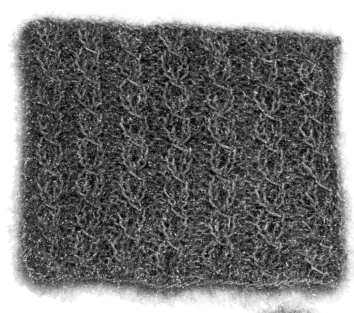

A cable variation that incorporates eyelets and doesn't use a cable needle.

Allover Cables

(Multiple of 6 sts + 2 sts)

Rows 1, 3, and 7: *P2, K4; rep from *, end P2.

Rows 2, 4, and 6: *K2, P4; rep from *, end K2.

Row 5: *P2, sl 2 sts to cn and hold in front, K2, K2 from cn; rep from *, end P2.

Row 8: *K2, P4; rep from *, end K2.

Rep rows 1–8.

Cables worked in an allover pattern.

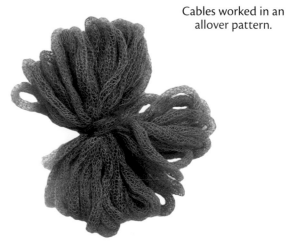

Chevron Stitches

Lots of energy grows from chevron stitches with their playful zigzags. Great for multicolored yarns, they show stripes in a new way. Whether you or the yarns add extra color, worked in either garter or stockinette stitch, chevrons give you good options for interest.

Large-Gauge Chevron Stitch

(Multiple of 10 sts + 3 sts)

Row 1: K1, ssk, *K3, YO, K1, YO, K3, sl 2-K1-p2sso; rep from *, end K3, YO, K1, YO, K3, K2tog, K1.

Row 2: Purl (for St st) or knit (for garter st).

Rep rows 1 and 2.

You can change the look of a single multicolored yarn in garter stitch (bottom) by switching to stockinette stitch and alternating every two rows with another yarn (top).

Garter Chevron

(Multiple of 16 sts + 3 sts)

Row 1: K1, *K1, YO, K6, sl 1-K2tog-psso, K6, YO; rep from *, end K2.

Row 2: K2, *P1, K13, P2; rep from *, end K1.

Rep rows 1 and 2.

Solid stripes banded with a multicolored texture add interest to this large garter chevron.

Color Work

The province of knitters and artists alike—using more than one color—provides the perfect enhancement to our blank canvas. Modern computer programs for charts and knitter's graph paper allow your color work to get as elaborate as you wish, but here is one simple way of working with color.

Fair Isle Stitch

(Multiple of 6 sts + 2 sts with yarns A and B)

Rows 1 and 3: K1 with B, *K3 with A, K3 with B; rep from *, end K1 with A.

Rows 2 and 4: P1 with A, *P3 with B, P3 with A; rep from *, end P1 with B.

Rows 5 and 7: K1 with A, *K3 with B, K3 with A; rep from *, end K1 with B.

Rows 6 and 8: P1 with B, *P3 with A, P3 with B; rep from*, end P1 with A.

Rep rows 1–8.

Yarn Creation

Become your own yarn designer! Knitting with more than one yarn held together throughout the garment lets you use even the thinnest yarns. Think thick and chunky; generally, the gauge is going to get larger and so will the needle. If you have a problem yarn, think about combining it with something else.

Worked in stockinette stitch, a soft furry nylon paired with a sparkly nylon improves both (bottom half). The fur softens both the look and hand of the sparkle, and together they are firmer than each is separately. The top half shows the switch to a nubby rayon instead of the sparkle.

Solid and multicolored yarns make the checkerboard appear and disappear.

What if I'm working in a stitch pattern and the pattern repeat does not match the template stitch numbers?

The template is a guide and not carved in stone. If the pattern repeat is six or fewer stitches, simply round up or down to the nearest number that works in the repeat. For example, the templates tell us the cast-on number is 70, and your repeat is 6. Total stitches (70) divided by repeat number (6) is 11.66 repeats. Round up to 12 repeats, multiply by 6, and the result (72 stitches) is the requirement for the repeat to work. Two stitches are not going to substantially change a garment's size. For larger repeats, look at how many additional or fewer stitches would be necessary to work in a full pattern repeat. Check this number against the stitch gauge to see how much larger or smaller the garment will be (you can do this easily by scanning across the first template row, finding the closest number, and noting the size). If moving to a new number is too much difference in size, try changing needle size in a new swatch. One needle size up or down may adjust the gauge enough so the multiple will now fit but won't jeopardize the feel of the knit piece.

Experiment when knitting your swatch: try creating half of a pattern repeat. It's very important to learn to read your knitting and not just the written pattern stitch. If you carefully watch what happens to the work as you create a row, you will see that for every action, there is a reaction. If you can visualize what the pattern wants you to do, it's easier to adjust a pattern or work only part of it so that patterns fit the desired stitch count.

Large pattern repeats require adapting numbers to work. Here, body ease was increased to accommodate pattern.

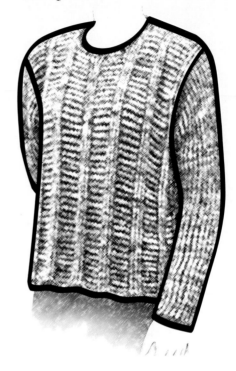

Smaller pattern repeats can be fitted more precisely since a few stitches won't alter the size much.

Working with the Templates

Your Guides to Great Knits

We're often asked if the templates are good for beginners. The answer is yes. If we had been taught to design with the templates, we would have become better knitters earlier in our lives. Coupling the templates with ever-improving knitting skills will help you learn to visualize and create the pieces needed to arrive at a finished garment that is what you intend. Most beginning knitters worry only about how to get stitches on the needle and keep them there. Novices don't necessarily need more to think about, but knitting is a simple process of working the same stitches over and over. Once you establish a knitting technique that works for you, the simple steps of watching your knitting's progress, checking gauge often to be sure you are consistent, and using a tape measure to ensure you are working to the right measurements will make you a more successful knitter. All of this comes from working with the templates. In short, our templates will make you a better knitter, one who is responsible for the quality of the garment you produce, and proud of it!

The templates are not gender or age specific. It's truly important when working with the templates to create a sketch of the garment you want to make. You can see from our design outlines that we offer ideas for multiple shapes and sizes, with different sleeve and neck options. As long as what you desire is on the template, then use the templates for sizes ranging from 30" to 60" in circumference. This will cover most adults and many older children, but not toddlers or babies.

For men or children, check the following measurements carefully.

✦ Shoulder width will probably be wider for men and may be narrower for children.

✦ Armhole depth will be deeper for men and may be smaller for children.

✦ Upper arm/sleeve width will probably be larger for men and may be smaller for children.

✦ If armhole depth changes, the cap length should increase or decrease to match.

Make these adjustments as needed, remembering that the templates were designed with women in mind.

The best part of working with *The New Knitter's Template* is that it makes you really think about the style and fit of the desired garment. We hope the tips and FAQs will start you on a journey where consequences become intentional rather than random. Never again will you search in vain for the perfect pattern with just the right details. The more you work with shaping specifically for you, the more comfortable you'll become with shaping pieces for a more perfect fit. You'll have confidence that the result of your hard work and hours spent knitting will be a successful garment you can actually wear! The more success you have, the bolder you will become, until designing your own sweaters will be second nature. Have at it!

I love to machine knit but finding good patterns is not easy. Can I use the templates to design for my knitting machine? FAQ

Designing for machine and hand knitting is essentially the same. Everything is based on a stitch/row gauge and measurements. Make sure to knit a very large gauge swatch on the machine; small machine knit pieces do not behave the same way as large ones (they get too narrow and stretch lengthwise). Keep track of your tension and feel free to try several different tension numbers on the same swatch. Mark the selvage where you change so you can accurately measure later. Block the swatch with steam before measuring since machine-knitted fabric must relax for accurate measurements to be taken. Once you know the stitch and row gauge, find the correct template and choose numbers as written for the body style you wish to create. Since the templates offer inches instead of row quantity for vertical measurements, you will have to multiply your row gauge by the desired measurement for a row count. You will fall in love with how easy it is to become a designer while using the templates: the numbers are right there for you. Envision your finished garment, make a gauge, find your template, find your size, and do the work—it is that simple.

I have been knitting for years and would like to write patterns for publication. Can I use the information on the templates to help size my designs?

The templates are there for everyone to use. You, as a designer, will decide specific style details and amounts of ease. The templates simply provide a shortcut to the math. When we write patterns for our own companies, we find our gauge template and select numbers for the multiple sizes for each pattern. Since we did the math once, it seems silly to redo it! Of course, you must double-check the numbers and adjust for stitch-pattern repeats. Be sure to know your fibers and how they will respond to the sizes you have selected. Part of a designer's responsibility is being in charge of how different yarns will work for different designs and sizes, and then altering them when necessary. The templates will give you numbers; the rest is up to you.

THE TEMPLATES

You've taken measurements and determined a size. You've also made a swatch with your selected yarn and know the appropriate gauge. Now, look through the following pages for your gauge and find the column with your size. Following the column down, enter the numbers for your size onto the "Blank Pattern Worksheet" (page 28) at the corresponding letters. Make any allowances for borders, pattern-stitch multiples, and adjustments for a custom fit. The swatch at the right side of each gauge chart is a full-size representation of the stitches per inch for that gauge.

Gauge *(6 sts x 8 rows = 1")*

Finished Bust/Chest	30	32	34	36	38	40	42
1/2 BODY (Back)							
A) CO Straight Body	90	96	102	108	114	120	126
A) CO Cropped Shape Taper	82	88	94	96	102	108	114
B) Inc 1 ea end every ___ rows ___ times	20/4	20/4	22/4	14/6	14/6	14/6	14/6
A) CO Fingertip Taper	100	106	112	120	126	132	138
C) Dec 1 ea end every ___" ___ times	3.5/5	3.5/5	3.5/5	3/6	3/6	3/6	3/6
A) CO Long Taper	118	124	130	138	144	150	156
C) Dec 1 ea end every ___" ___ times	2/14	2/14	2/14	1.5/15	1.5/15	1.5/15	1.5/15
SHAPE ARMHOLE							
Cut In (sleeveless)							
E) BO ___ sts beg next ___ rows	4/2	5/2	6/2	7/2	8/2	8/2	9/2
F) Dec 1 ea end EOR ___ times	4	5	5	6	7	8	9
G) Dec 1 ea end every 4th row ___ times	4	5	5	6	7	8	9
Set In							
E) BO ___ sts beg next ___ rows	4/2	5/2	5/2	7/2	8/2	9/2	5/4
F) Dec 1 ea end EOR ___ times	3	4	5	6	7	9	9
Modified Drop							
H) BO ___ sts beg next 2 rows	3	6	6	9	9	12	12
1/2 BODY (Pullover Front)							
Boatneck: (J) BO ctr ___ sts	48	48	48	48	50	52	52
Round Neck Shaping							
K) BO ctr ___ sts	14	14	16	18	20	20	22
L) BO ___ sts ea neck edge 1 time	3	3	3	3	3	3	3
M) BO ___ sts ea neck edge 1 time	2	2	2	2	2	2	2
N) Dec 1 ea neck edge EOR ___ times	3	3	3	3	3	3	3
Deep V: Dec ea neck edge							
O) every ___ rows ___ times	4/15	4/15	3/16	3/17	3/18	3/18	3/18
Shallow V: Dec ea neck edge							
O) every ___ rows ___ times	2/15	2/15	2/16	2/17	2/18	2/18	2/18
1/2 FRONT (Cardigan/Jkt)							
P) CO Straight Shape	45	48	51	54	57	60	63
P) CO Fingertip Taper	50	53	56	60	63	66	69
Q) Dec 1 at side edge every ___" ___ times	3.5/5	3.5/5	3.5/5	3/6	3/6	3/6	3/6
P) CO Long Taper	59	62	65	69	72	75	78
Q) Dec 1 at side edge every ___" ___ times	2/14	2/14	2/14	1.5/15	1.5/15	1.5/15	1.5/15
Round Neck Shaping							
R) BO ___ sts beg next row	7	7	8	9	10	10	10
Follow shaping (L, M, N) from above at neck edge only							
SLEEVES							
S) CO Long Sleeve	36	38	40	42	42	44	46
T) Inc 1 ea end every ___ rows ___ times	5/21	5/21	5/21	5/21	5/22	5/22	5/22
S) CO Short Sleeve	60	62	64	66	68	70	72
T) Inc 1 ea end every ___ rows ___ times	3/9	3/9	3/9	3/9	3/9	3/9	3/9
S) CO Cap Sleeve	72	74	76	78	80	82	84
T) Inc 1 ea end every ___ rows ___ times	3/3	3/3	3/3	3/3	4/3	4/3	4/3
CAP SHAPING							
Set In							
U) BO ___ sts beg next 2 rows	4	5	5	7	8	9	5
V) Dec 1 ea end EOR for ___"	4	4	4	4.5	4.5	4.5	5
Modified Drop							
W) BO ___ sts beg every row ___ times	2/24	2/24	2/24	2/24	3/24	2/24	2/24

44	46	48	50	52	54	56	58	60
132	138	144	150	156	162	168	174	180
120	124	130	136	142	148	154	160	166
14/6	12/7	12/7	12/7	12/7	12/7	12/7	12/7	12/7
144	154	160	166	172	178	184	190	196
3/6	2/8	2/8	2/8	2/8	2/8	2/8	2.5/8	2.5/8
162	172	178	184	190	196	204	210	216
2/15	1.5/17	1.5/17	1.5/17	1.5/17	1.5/17	1.5/18	1.5/18	1.5/18
7/4	7/4	8/4	9/4	7/6	7/6	8/6	9/6	9/6
8	9	9	9	9	10	10	9	11
8	8	9	9	9	9	9	9	10
6/4	6/4	7/4	7/4	7/4	8/4	8/4	9/4	9/4
9	10	10	11	13	12	15	15	18
15	15	15	15	18	18	21	21	24
54	54	54	56	56	58	58	60	60
22	24	24	26	26	26	26	26	26
3	3	3	3	3	3	3	3	3
2	2	2	2	2	2	2	2	2
3	3	3	3	3	3	3	3	3
3/19	3/20	3/20	3/21	3/21	3/21	3/21	3/21	3/21
2/19	2/20	2/20	2/21	2/21	2/21	2/21	2/21	2/21
66	69	72	75	78	81	84	87	90
72	77	80	83	86	89	92	95	98
3/6	2/8	2/8	2/8	2/8	2/8	2/8	2.5/8	2.5/8
81	86	89	92	95	98	102	105	108
2/15	1.5/17	1.5/17	1.5/17	1.5/17	1.5/17	1.5/18	1.5/18	1.5/18
11	12	12	13	13	13	13	13	13
48	50	52	54	54	54	54	54	54
5/23	5/23	5/23	5/23	5/24	5/25	5/26	5/22	5/27
74	76	78	80	82	84	86	88	90
3/10	3/10	4/10	4/10	4/10	4/10	4/10	4/10	4/10
86	88	90	92	94	94	96	96	96
3/4	3/4	3/4	4/4	4/4	3/5	3/5	3/6	3/6
6	6	7	7	7	8	8	9	9
5	5	5.5	5.5	5.5	6	6	6.5	6.5
3/24	3/24	3/24	3/24	3/24	3/24	3/24	3/24	3/24

Gauge *(5.5 sts x 7.5 rows = 1")*

Finished Bust/Chest	30	32	34	36	38	40	42
1/2 BODY (Back)							
A) CO Straight Body	82	88	94.	100	104	110	116
A) CO Cropped Shape Taper	74	80	86	90	94	100	104
B) Inc 1 ea end every ___ rows ___ times	18/4	18/4	20/4	14/5	14/5	14/5	12/6
A) CO Fingertip Taper	90	96	102	110	114	120	128
C) Dec 1 ea end every ___" ___ times	4/4	4/4	4/4	3.5/5	3.5/5	3.5/5	3/6
A) CO Long Taper	106	112	118	126	130	138	144
C) Dec 1 ea end every ___" ___ times	2/12	2/12	2/12	2/13	2/13	2/14	2/14
SHAPE ARMHOLE							
Cut In (sleeveless)							
E) BO ___ sts beg next ___ rows	5/2	5/2	6/2	6/2	6/2	6/2	7/2
F) Dec 1 ea end EOR ___ times	3	5	5	6	7	8	10
G) Dec 1 ea end every 4th row ___ times	3	4	4	6	7	8	8
Set In							
E) BO ___ sts beg next ___ rows	5/2	5/2	5/2	5/2	5/2	6/2	6/2
F) Dec 1 ea end EOR ___ times	2	3	4	7	8	10	12
Modified Drop							
H) BO ___ sts beg next 2 rows	3	5	6	8	8	11	11
1/2 BODY (Pullover Front)							
Boatneck: (J) BO ctr ___ sts	44	44	44	44	46	46	48
Round Neck Shaping							
K) BO ctr ___ sts	12	14	14	14	16	16	18
L) BO ___ sts ea neck edge 1 time	3	3	3	3	3	3	3
M) BO ___ sts ea neck edge 1 time	2	2	3	3	3	3	3
N) Dec 1 ea neck edge EOR ___ times	2	2	2	2	2	2	2
Deep V: Dec ea neck edge							
O) every ___ rows ___ times	4/13	4/14	4/15	4/15	4/16	4/16	3/17
Shallow V: Dec ea neck edge							
O) every ___ rows ___ times	2/13	2/14	2/15	2/15	2/16	2/16	2/17
1/2 FRONT (Cardigan/Jkt)							
P) CO Straight Shape	41	44	47	50	52	55	58
P) CO Fingertip Taper	45	48	51	55	57	60	64
Q) Dec 1 at side edge every ___" ___ times	4/4	4/4	4/4	3.5/5	3.5/5	3.5/5	3/6
P) CO Long Taper	53	56	59	63	65	69	72
Q) Dec 1 at side edge every ___" ___ times	2/12	2/12	2/12	2/13	2/13	2/14	2/14
Round Neck Shaping							
R) BO ___ sts beg next row	6	7	7	7	8	8	9
Follow shaping (L, M, N) from above at neck edge only							
SLEEVES							
S) CO Long Sleeve	30	32	34	36	36	38	40
T) Inc 1 ea end every ___ rows ___ times	5/20	5/20	5/20	5/20	5/21	5/21	5/21
S) CO Short Sleeve	54	56	58	60	62	64	66
T) Inc 1 ea end every ___ rows ___ times	3/8	3/8	3/8	3/8	3/8	3/8	3/8
S) CO Cap Sleeve	64	66	68	70	72	74	76
T) Inc 1 ea end every ___ rows ___ times	3/3	3/3	3/3	3/3	4/3	4/3	4/3
CAP SHAPING							
Set In							
U) BO ___ sts beg next 2 rows	5	5	5	5	5	6	6
V) Dec 1 ea end EOR for ___"	4	4	4	4.5	4.5	4.5	5
Modified Drop							
W) BO ___ sts beg every row ___ times	2/22	2/22	2/22	2/22	2/22	2/22	2/22

44	46	48	50	52	54	56	58	60
120	126	132	138	142	148	154	160	166
108	112	118	124	128	134	140	146	152
12/6	12/7	12/7	12/7	12/7	12/7	12/7	12/7	12/7
132	140	146	152	156	162	168	174	180
3/6	2.5/7	2.5/7	2.5/7	2.5/7	2.5/7	2.5/7	2.5/7	2.5/7
148	156	162	168	172	180	186	192	198
2/14	2/15	2/15	2/15	2/15	2/16	2/16	2/16	2/16
5/4	5/4	6/4	7/4	7/4	7/4	8/4	8/4	8/4
10	11	15	14	17	20	22	25	27
7	7	5	5	4	3	2	1	1
6/2	4/4	4/4	5/4	5/4	6/4	6/4	7/4	7/4
13	12	14	14	14	14	17	17	19
13	13	14	14	16	16	19	20	23
48	50	50	52	52	54	54	56	56
20	20	20	20	20	20	20	20	20
3	3	3	3	3	3	3	3	3
3	3	3	3	3	3	3	3	3
2	2	2	3	3	3	3	3	3
3/18	3/18	3/18	3/19	3/19	3/19	3/19	4/19	4/19
2/18	2/18	2/18	2/19	2/19	2/19	2/19	2/19	2/19
60	63	66	69	71	74	77	80	83
66	70	73	76	78	81	84	87	90
3/6	2.5/7	2.5/7	2.5/7	2.5/7	2.5/7	2.5/7	2.5/7	2.5/7
74	78	81	84	86	90	93	96	99
2/14	2/15	2/15	2/15	2/15	2/16	2/16	2/16	2/16
10	10	10	10	10	10	10	10	10
42	44	44	46	48	50	50	50	50
5/21	5/21	5/22	5/22	5/22	5/22	5/23	5/24	5/25
68	70	72	76	78	80	82	84	84
3/8	3/8	3/8	4/7	4/7	4/7	4/7	4/7	4/8
78	80	82	84	86	88	88	90	90
4/3	4/3	5/3	5/3	5/3	5/3	5/4	5/4	4/5
6	4	4	5	5	6	6	7	7
5	5	5.5	5.5	5.5	6	6	6.5	6.5
3/22	3/22	3/22	3/22	3/24	3/24	3/24	3/24	3/24

Gauge *(5 sts x 7.5 rows = 1")*

Finished Bust/Chest	30	32	34	36	38	40	42
1/2 BODY (Back)							
A) CO Straight Body	76	80	86	90	96	100	106
A) CO Cropped Shape Taper	68	72	78	80	86	90	96
B) Inc 1 ea end every ___ rows ___ times	18/4	18/4	20/4	14/5	14/5	14/5	14/5
A) CO Fingertip Taper	84	88	94	100	106	110	116
C) Dec 1 ea end every ___" ___ times	4/4	4/4	4/4	3.5/5	3.5/5	3.5/5	3.5/5
A) CO Long Taper	98	102	108	114	120	124	130
C) Dec 1 ea end every ___" ___ times	2.5/11	2.5/11	2.5/11	2/12	2.5/12	2.5/12	2.5/12
SHAPE ARMHOLE							
Cut In (sleeveless)							
E) BO ___ sts beg next ___ rows	4/2	4/2	5/2	5/2	6/2	6/2	7/2
F) Dec 1 ea end EOR ___ times	4	4	5	6	7	7	8
G) Dec 1 ea end every 4th row ___ times	3	4	4	5	6	7	8
Set In							
E) BO ___ sts beg next ___ rows	3/2	4/2	4/2	5/2	5/2	5/2	6/2
F) Dec 1 ea end EOR ___ times	4	4	5	6	8	10	11
Modified Drop							
H) BO ___ sts beg next 2 rows	3	5	6	8	8	10	10
1/2 BODY (Pullover Front)							
Boatneck: (J) BO ctr ___ sts	40	40	40	40	42	42	44
Round Neck Shaping							
K) BO ctr ___ sts	10	12	12	14	14	14	14
L) BO ___ sts ea neck edge 1 time	3	3	3	3	3	3	3
M) BO ___ sts ea neck edge 1 time	2	2	2	2	3	3	3
N) Dec 1 ea neck edge EOR ___ times	2	2	2	2	2	2	2
Deep V: Dec ea neck edge							
O) every ___ rows ___ times	4/12	4/13	4/13	4/14	4/15	4/15	4/15
Shallow V: Dec ea neck edge							
O) every ___ rows ___ times	2/12	2/13	2/13	2/14	2/15	2/15	2/15
1/2 FRONT (Cardigan/Jkt)							
P) CO Straight Shape	38	40	43	45	48	50	53
P) CO Fingertip Taper	42	44	47	50	53	55	58
Q) Dec 1 at side edge every ___" ___ times	4/4	4/4	4/4	3.5/5	3.5/5	3.5/5	3.5/5
P) CO Long Taper	49	51	54	57	60	62	65
Q) Dec 1 at side edge every ___" ___ times	2.5/11	2.5/11	2.5/11	2/12	2.5/12	2.5/12	2.5/12
Round Neck Shaping							
R) BO ___ sts beg next row	5	6	6	7	7	7	7
Follow shaping (L, M, N) from above at neck edge only							
SLEEVES							
S) CO Long Sleeve	30	30	30	32	34	34	36
T) Inc 1 ea end every ___ rows ___ times	6/17	6/18	6/19	6/19	6/19	6/20	6/20
S) CO Short Sleeve	50	52	54	56	58	60	62
T) Inc 1 ea end every ___ rows ___ times	4/7	4/7	4/7	4/7	4/7	4/7	4/7
S) CO Cap Sleeve	60	62	64	66	68	70	72
T) Inc 1 ea end every ___ rows ___ times	4/2	4/2	4/2	4/2	6/2	6/2	6/2
CAP SHAPING							
Set In							
U) BO ___ sts beg next 2 rows	3	4	4	5	5	5	6
V) Dec 1 ea end EOR for ___"	4	4	4	4.5	4.5	4.5	5
Modified Drop							
W) BO ___ sts beg every row ___ times	2/20	2/20	2/22	2/22	2/22	2/22	3/22

44	46	48	50	52	54	56	58	60
110	116	120	126	130	136	140	146	150
100	104	108	114	118	124	128	134	138
16/5	14/6	14/6	14/6	14/6	12/6	12/6	12/6	12/6
120	128	132	138	142	148	152	158	162
3.5/5	3/6	3/6	3/6	3/6	3/6	3/6	3/6	3/6
134	144	148	154	158	164	170	176	180
2.5/12	2.5/14	2/14	2/14	2/14	2/14	2/15	2/15	2/15
4/4	4/4	5/4	5/4	6/4	6/4	7/4	7/4	8/4
9	12	14	17	18	21	20	22	22
8	7	5	4	3	2	2	2	2
6/2	4/4	4/4	5/4	5/4	6/4	6/4	7/4	7/4
12	11	12	12	13	13	14	14	16
12	13	13	13	15	15	17	18	20
44	46	46	48	48	48	50	50	50
16	16	16	16	16	16	18	18	18
3	3	3	3	3	3	3	3	3
3	3	3	3	3	3	3	3	3
2	2	2	3	3	3	3	3	3
4/16	4/16	4/16	3/17	3/17	3/17	3/18	3/18	3/18
2/16	2/16	2/16	2/17	2/17	2/17	2/18	2/18	2/18
55	58	60	63	65	68	70	73	75
60	64	66	69	71	74	76	79	81
3.5/5	3/6	3/6	3/6	3/6	3/6	3/6	3/6	3/6
67	72	74	77	79	82	85	88	90
2.5/12	2.5/14	2/14	2/14	2/14	2/14	2/15	2/15	2/15
8	8	8	8	8	8	9	9	9
38	40	40	42	42	44	44	46	48
6/20	6/20	6/20	6/21	5/22	5/22	5/23	5/23	5/23
64	66	66	68	70	72	74	76	76
4/7	4/7	4/7	4/8	4/8	4/8	4/8	4/8	4/9
74	76	76	78	80	82	84	86	86
6/2	6/2	8/2	6/3	6/3	6/3	6/3	6/3	4/4
6	4	4	5	5	6	6	7	7
5	5	5.5	5.5	5.5	6	6	6.5	6.5
3/22	3/22	3/22	3/22	3/24	3/24	3/24	3/24	3/24

Gauge *(4.5 sts x 7 rows = 1")*

Finished Bust/Chest	30	32	34	36	38	40	42
1/2 BODY (Back)							
A) CO Straight Body	68	72	76	82	86	90	94
A) CO Cropped Shape Taper	60	64	68	72	76	80	84
B) Inc 1 ea end every ___ rows ___ times	16/4	16/4	16/4	14/5	14/5	14/5	14/5
A) CO Fingertip Taper	74	78	82	90	94	98	102
C) Dec 1 ea end every ___" ___ times	6/3	6/3	6/3	4.5/4	4.5/4	4.5/4	4.5/4
A) CO Long Taper	88	92	96	104	108	112	116
C) Dec 1 ea end every ___" ___ times	2.5/10	2.5/10	2.5/10	2.5/11	2.5/11	2.5/11	2.5/11
SHAPE ARMHOLE							
Cut In (sleeveless)							
E) BO ___ sts beg next ___ rows	4/2	5/2	5/2	5/2	5/2	5/2	5/2
F) Dec 1 ea end EOR ___ times	3	3	4	5	6	7	8
G) Dec 1 ea end every 4th row ___ times	2	3	3	5	6	6	7
Set In							
E) BO ___ sts beg next ___ rows	3/2	4/2	4/2	5/2	5/2	5/2	5/2
F) Dec 1 ea end EOR ___ times	3	3	4	6	7	9	10
Modified Drop							
H) BO ___ sts beg next 2 rows	3	4	4	7	7	9	9
1/2 BODY (Pullover Front)							
Boatneck: (J) BO ctr ___ sts	36	36	36	36	38	38	40
Round Neck Shaping							
K) BO ctr ___ sts	10	10	12	12	12	12	14
L) BO ___ sts ea neck edge 1 time	3	3	3	3	3	3	3
M) BO ___ sts ea neck edge 1 time	2	2	2	2	3	2	2
N) Dec 1 ea neck edge EOR ___ times	1	1	1	1	2	2	2
Deep V: Dec ea neck edge							
O) every ___ rows ___ times	4/11	4/11	4/12	4/12	4/13	4/13	4/14
Shallow V: Dec ea neck edge							
O) every ___ rows ___ times	2/11	2/11	2/12	3/12	2/13	2/13	2/14
1/2 FRONT (Cardigan/Jkt)							
P) CO Straight Shape	34	36	38	41	43	45	47
P) CO Fingertip Taper	37	39	41	45	47	49	51
Q) Dec 1 at side edge every ___" ___ times	6/3	6/3	6/3	4.5/4	4.5/4	4.5/4	4.5/4
P) CO Long Taper	44	46	48	52	54	56	58
Q) Dec 1 at side edge every ___" ___ times	2.5/10	2.5/10	2.5/10	2.5/11	2.5/11	2.5/11	2.5/11
Round Neck Shaping							
R) BO ___ sts beg next row	11	11	12	12	13	13	14
Follow shaping (L, M, N) from above at neck edge only							
SLEEVES							
S) CO Long Sleeve	26	28	28	30	32	32	34
T) Inc 1 ea end every ___ rows ___ times	6/16	6/16	6/17	6/17	6/17	6/18	6/18
S) CO Short Sleeve	44	46	48	50	52	54	56
T) Inc 1 ea end every ___ rows ___ times	4/7	4/7	4/7	4/7	4/7	4/7	4/7
S) CO Cap Sleeve	54	56	58	60	62	64	66
T) Inc 1 ea end every ___ rows ___ times	4/2	4/2	4/2	4/2	6/2	6/2	6/2
CAP SHAPING							
Set In							
U) BO ___ sts beg next 2 rows	3	4	4	5	5	5	5
V) Dec 1 ea end EOR for ___"	4	4	4	4.5	4.5	4.5	5
Modified Drop							
W) BO ___ sts beg every row ___ times	2/20	2/20	2/20	2/20	2/20	2/20	2/20

44	46	48	50	52	54	56	58	60
100	104	108	112	118	122	126	130	136
90	94	98	102	108	112	116	120	126
14/5	14/5	14/5	14/5	14/5	14/5	14/5	14/5	14/5
110	114	118	122	128	132	136	140	146
4/5	4/5	4/5	4/5	4/5	4/5	4/5	4/5	4/5
124	128	134	138	144	148	154	158	164
2.5/12	2.5/12	2/13	2/13	2/13	2.5/13	2/14	2/14	2/14
4/4	5/4	5/4	5/4	6/4	6/4	6/6	6/6	6/6
8	7	9	9	11	12	8	8	10
7	7	8	8	7	7	7	8	8
6/2	6/2	5/4	5/4	5/4	6/4	6/4	6/4	6/4
10	11	8	9	10	10	12	13	15
11	12	11	11	14	13	15	15	18
40	40	40	42	42	44	44	46	46
14	14	14	14	14	14	16	16	16
3	3	3	3	3	3	3	3	3
2	3	3	3	3	3	3	3	3
2	2	2	2	3	3	3	3	3
4/14	4/15	4/15	4/15	4/16	4/16	4/17	4/17	4/17
2/14	2/15	2/15	2/15	2/16	2/16	2/17	2/17	2/17
50	52	54	56	59	61	63	65	68
55	57	59	61	64	66	68	70	73
4.5/4	3/6	3/6	3/6	3/6	3.5/6	3.5/6	2.5/6	3.5/6
62	64	67	69	72	74	77	79	82
2.5/12	2.5/12	2/13	2/13	2/13	2.5/13	2/14	2/14	2/14
14	15	15	15	16	16	17	17	17
36	36	38	40	40	40	42	42	42
6/18	6/18	6/18	6/18	5/19	5/20	5/20	5/21	5/22
58	58	60	62	64	66	68	70	72
4/7	4/7	4/7	4/7	4/7	4/7	4/7	4/7	4/7
68	68	70	72	74	76	78	80	82
6/2	6/2	6/2	6/2	6/2	6/2	6/2	6/2	6/2
6	6	5	5	5	6	6	6	6
5	5	5.5	5.5	5.5	6	6	6.5	6.5
2/20	2/20	3/20	3/20	3/20	3/20	3/20	3/20	3/20

Gauge *(4 sts x 6.5 rows = 1")*

Finished Bust/Chest	30	32	34	36	38	40	42
1/2 BODY (Back)							
A) CO Straight Body	60	64	68	72	76	80	84
A) CO Cropped Shape Taper	54	58	62	64	68	72	76
B) Inc 1 ea end every ___ rows ___ times	20/3	20/3	20/3	14/4	14/4	14/4	14/4
A) CO Fingertip Taper	66	70	74	80	84	88	92
C) Dec 1 ea end every ___" ___ times	5.5/3	5.5/8	6/3	4.5/4	4.5/4	4.5/4	4.5/4
A) CO Long Taper	78	82	86	92	96	100	104
C) Dec 1 ea end every ___" ___ times	3/9	3/9	3.5/9	2.5/10	2.5/10	2.5/10	2.5/10
SHAPE ARMHOLE							
Cut In (sleeveless)							
E) BO ___ sts beg next ___ rows	3/2	4/2	4/2	5/2	5/2	6/2	6/2
F) Dec 1 ea end EOR ___ times	3	3	4	4	5	5	6
G) Dec 1 ea end every 4th row ___ times	2	3	3	4	5	5	6
Set In							
E) BO ___ sts beg next ___ rows	3/2	3/2	3/2	4/2	5/2	5/2	6/2
F) Dec 1 ea end EOR ___ times	2	3	4	5	5	7	7
Modified Drop							
H) BO ___ sts beg next 2 rows	2	4	4	6	6	8	8
1/2 BODY (Pullover Front)							
Boatneck: (J) BO ctr ___sts	32	32	32	32	34	34	34
Round Neck Shaping							
K) BO ctr ___ sts	6	6	8	8	10	10	10
L) BO ___ sts ea neck edge 1 time	3	3	3	3	3	3	3
M) BO ___ sts ea neck edge 1 time	2	2	2	2	2	2	2
N) Dec 1 ea neck edge EOR ___ times	2	2	2	2	2	2	2
Deep V: Dec ea neck edge							
O) every ___ rows ___ times	4/10	4/10	4/11	4/11	4/12	4/12	4/13
Shallow V: Dec ea neck edge							
O) every ___ rows ___ times	3/10	3/10	3/11	3/11	3/12	3/12	3/12
1/2 FRONT (Cardigan/Jkt)							
P) CO Straight Shape	30	32	34	36	38	40	42
P) CO Fingertip Taper	33	35	37	40	42	44	46
Q) Dec 1 at side edge every ___" ___ times	5.5/3	5.5/3	6/3	4.5/4	4.5/4	4.5/4	4.5/4
P) CO Long Taper	39	41	43	46	48	50	52
Q) Dec 1 at side edge every ___" ___ times	3/9	3/9	3.5/9	2.5/10	2.5/10	2.5/10	2.5/10
Round Neck Shaping							
R) BO ___ sts beg next row	3	3	4	4	5	5	5
Follow shaping (L, M, N) from above at neck edge only							
SLEEVES							
S) CO Long Sleeve	24	24	24	28	28	28	28
T) Inc 1 ea end every ___ rows ___ times	6/14	6/14	6/16	6/14	6/14	6/16	6/16
S) CO Short Sleeve	40	40	44	44	44	48	48
T) Inc 1 ea end every ___ rows ___ times	4/6	4/6	4/6	4/6	4/6	4/6	4/6
S) CO Cap Sleeve	48	48	52	52	52	56	56
T) Inc 1 ea end every ___ rows ___ times	4/2	4/2	4/2	4/2	4/2	4/2	4/2
CAP SHAPING							
Set In							
U) BO ___ sts beg next 2 rows	3	3	3	4	5	5	6
V) Dec 1 ea end EOR for ___"	4	4	4	4.5	4.5	4.5	5
Modified Drop							
W) BO ___ sts beg every row ___ times	2/20	2/20	2/20	2/20	2/20	2/20	2/20

44	46	48	50	52	54	56	58	60
88	92	96	100	104	108	112	116	120
80	82	86	90	94	98	102	106	110
14/4	12/5	12/5	12/5	12/5	12/5	12/5	12/5	12/5
96	102	106	110	114	118	122	126	130
4.5/4	4/5	4/5	4/5	4/5	4/5	4/5	4.5/5	4.5/5
108	114	118	122	126	130	136	140	144
3/10	2.5/11	2.5/11	3/11	3/11	3/11	2.5/12	3/12	3/12
6/2	7/2	4/4	4/4	4/4	5/4	6/4	6/4	7/4
7	7	8	8	10	9	9	9	10
7	7	7	8	8	8	8	9	9
6/2	6/2	4/4	4/4	5/4	5/4	6/4	6/4	7/4
8	9	8	9	8	9	9	10	10
10	10	10	10	12	12	14	14	16
36	36	36	38	38	38	38	40	40
10	12	12	12	12	12	12	12	12
3	3	3	3	3	3	3	3	3
2	2	2	2	2	2	2	2	2
2	2	2	2	3	3	3	3	3
4/12	4/13	4/13	4/13	4/14	4/14	4/14	4/14	4/14
3/12	2/13	2/13	2/13	2/14	2/14	2/14	2/14	2/14
44	46	48	50	52	54	56	58	60
48	51	53	55	57	59	61	63	65
4.5/4	4/5	4/5	4/5	4/5	4/5	4/5	4.5/5	4.5/5
54	57	59	61	63	65	68	70	72
3/10	2.5/11	2.5/11	3/11	3/11	3/11	2.5/12	3/12	3/12
5	6	6	6	6	6	6	6	6
32	32	32	36	36	36	36	36	36
6/16	6/16	6/16	6/16	6/16	6/16	6/18	6/18	6/18
52	52	52	56	56	56	60	60	60
4/6	4/6	4/6	4/6	4/6	4/6	4/6	4/6	4/6
60	60	60	64	64	64	64	60	64
4/2	4/2	6/2	6/2	6/2	6/2	4/4	4/4	4/4
6	6	4	4	5	5	6	6	7
5	5	5.5	5.5	5.5	6	6	6.5	6.5
3/18	3/18	3/18	3/18	3/18	3/18	3/18	3/18	3/18

Gauge *(3.5 sts x 5 rows = 1")*

Finished Bust/Chest	30	32	34	36	38	40	42
1/2 BODY (Back)							
A) CO Straight Body	52	56	60	64	66	70	74
A) CO Cropped Shape Taper	48	50	54	56	60	64	66
B) Inc 1 ea end every ___ rows ___ times	24/2	18/3	20/3	14/4	20/3	20/3	14/4
A) CO Fingertip Taper	58	62	66	70	74	78	80
C) Dec 1 ea end every ___" ___ times	6/3	6/3	6/3	6/3	5/4	5/4	6/3
A) CO Long Taper	68	72	76	80	84	88	92
C) Dec 1 ea end every ___" ___ times	3/8	3/8	3/8	3/8	3/8	3/9	3/9
SHAPE ARMHOLE							
Cut In (sleeveless)							
E) BO ___ sts beg next ___ rows.	3/2	3/2	4/2	4/2	5/2	5/2	3/4
F) Dec 1 ea end EOR ___ times	2	3	3	4	4	5	5
G) Dec 1 ea end every 4th row ___ times	2	3	3	4	4	4	5
Set In							
E) BO ___ sts beg next ___ rows	2/2	2/2	3/2	4/2	4/2	5/2	5/2
F) Dec 1 ea end EOR ___ times	2	3	3	4	4	5	7
Modified Drop							
H) BO ___ sts beg next 2 rows	2	3	4	6	5	7	7
1/2 BODY (Pullover Front)							
Boatneck: (J) BO ctr ___ sts	28	28	28	28	30	30	32
Round Neck Shaping							
K) BO ctr ___ sts	8	8	10	10	10	10	10
L) BO ___ sts ea neck edge 1 time	2	2	2	2	3	3	3
M) BO ___ sts ea neck edge 1 time	2	2	2	2	2	2	2
N) Dec 1 ea neck edge EOR ___ times	1	1	1	1	1	1	1
Deep V: Dec ea neck edge							
O) every ___ rows ___ times	4/9	4/9	4/10	4/10	4/11	4/11	4/11
Shallow V: Dec ea neck edge							
O) every ___ rows ___ times	2/9	2/9	2/10	2/10	2/11	2/11	2/11
1/2 FRONT (Cardigan/Jkt)							
P) CO Straight Shape	26	28	30	32	33	35	37
P) CO Fingertip Taper	29	31	33	35	37	39	40
Q) Dec 1 at side edge every ___" ___ times	6/3	6/3	6/3	6/3	5/4	5/4	6/3
P) CO Long Taper	34	36	38	40	42	44	46
Q) Dec 1 at side edge every ___" ___ times	3/8	3/8	3/8	3/8	3/9	3/9	3/9
Round Neck Shaping							
R) BO ___ sts beg next row	4	4	5	5	5	5	6
Follow shaping (L, M, N) from above at neck edge only							
SLEEVES							
S) CO Long Sleeve	22	22	22	24	24	24	24
T) Inc 1 ea end every ___ rows ___ times	6/12	6/12	6/13	6/13	6/13	6/14	6/14
S) CO Short Sleeve	36	36	38	38	38	40	42
T) Inc 1 ea end every ___ rows ___ times	4/5	4/5	4/5	3/6	3/6	3/6	4/5
S) CO Cap Sleeve	42	42	44	46	46	48	48
T) Inc 1 ea end every ___ rows ___ times	3/2	3/2	3/2	3/2	4/2	4/2	4/2
CAP SHAPING							
Set In							
U) BO ___ sts beg next 2 rows	2	2	3	4	4	5	5
V) Dec 1 ea end EOR for ___"	4	4	4	4.5	4.5	4.5	5
Modified Drop							
W) BO ___ sts beg every row ___ times	2/16	2/16	2/16	2/16	2/16	2/16	2/16

44	46	48	50	52	54	56	58	60
78	80	84	88	92	94	98	102	106
70	72	76	78	82	86	90	94	96
14/4	14/4	14/4	14/5	14/5	14/4	14/4	14/4	12/5
84	88	92	96	100	104	106	110	114
6/3	5/4	5/4	5/4	5/4	4/5	5/4	5/4	5/4
94	100	104	106	110	114	118	122	126
3.5/8	3/10	3/10	3/9	3.5/9	3/10	3.5/10	3/10	3.5/10
4/4	4/4	5/4	5/4	5/4	5/4	6/4	4/6	5/6
5	5	5	6	6	8	8	9	8
5	5	5	5	5	5	5	5	5
5/2	5/2	5/2	5/2	3/4	3/4	4/4	4/4	5/4
8	8	9	10	10	10	10	11	11
9	8	9	9	11	11	12	12	14
32	32	32	34	34	34	34	36	36
10	10	10	12	12	12	12	12	12
3	3	3	3	3	3	3	3	3
2	2	2	2	2	2	2	2	2
1	1	1	1	1	1	1	1	1
4/11	4/11	4/11	4/12	4/12	4/12	4/12	4/12	4/12
2/11	2/11	2/11	2/12	2/12	2/12	2/12	2/12	2/12
39	40	42	44	46	47	49	51	53
42	44	46	48	50	52	53	55	57
6/3	5/4	5/4	5/4	5/4	4/5	5/4	5/4	5/4
47	50	52	53	55	57	59	61	63
3.5/8	3/10	3/10	3/9	3.5/9	3/10	3.5/10	3/10	3.5/10
6	5	5	6	6	6	6	6	6
26	28	28	30	30	32	32	32	32
6/14	6/14	6/14	6/14	5/15	6/14	6/15	5/16	5/16
44	46	46	48	50	50	52	52	52
4/5	4/5	4/5	4/5	4/5	4/5	5/5	4/6	4/6
50	52	52	54	56	56	56	58	58
4/2	4/2	5/2	5/2	5/2	5/2	4/3	4/3	4/3
5	5	5	5	3	3	4	4	5
5	5	5.5	5.5	5.5	6	6	6.5	6.5
2/16	2/16	2/16	2/16	2/16	2/16	3/16	3/16	3/16

71

Gauge *(3 sts x 5 rows = 1")*

Finished Bust/Chest	30	32	34	36	38	40	42
1/2 BODY (Back)							
A) CO Straight Body	46	48	52	54	58	60	64
A) CO Cropped Shape Taper	40	44	46	48	52	54	58
B) Inc 1 ea end every ___ rows ___ times	17/3	22/2	16/3	16/3	16/3	16/3	16/3
A) CO Fingertip Taper	50	52	56	60	64	66	70
C) Dec 1 ea end every ___" ___ times	8.5/2	8.5/2	9/2	6/3	6.5/3	6/3	6/3
A) CO Long Taper	58	62	64	68	72	76	78
C) Dec 1 ea end every ___" ___ times	4.5/6	4/7	5/6	4/7	4/7	3.5/8	4/7
SHAPE ARMHOLE							
Cut In (Sleeveless)							
E) BO ___ sts beg next ___ rows	2/2	3/2	3/2	3/2	4/2	4/2	4/2
F) Dec 1 ea end EOR ___ times	2	2	3	4	4	4	5
G) Dec 1 ea end every 4th row ___ times	2	2	3	3	4	4	5
Set In							
E) BO ___ sts beg next ___ rows	2/2	2/2	2/2	3/2	3/2	3/2	4/2
F) Dec 1 ea end EOR ___ times	2	2	4	4	5	6	6
Modified Drop							
H) BO ___ sts beg next 2 rows	2	3	3	4	5	6	6
1/2 BODY (Pullover Front)							
Boatneck: (J) BO ctr ___ sts	24	24	24	24	26	26	26
Round Neck Shaping							
K) BO ctr ___ sts	6	6	6	6	8	8	8
L) BO ___ sts ea neck edge 1 time	2	2	2	2	2	2	2
M) BO ___ sts ea neck edge 1 time	2	2	2	2	2	2	2
N) Dec 1 ea neck edge EOR ___ times	1	1	1	1	1	1	1
Deep V: Dec ea neck edge							
O) every ___ rows ___ times	4/8	4/8	4/8	4/8	4/9	4/9	4/9
Shallow V: Dec ea neck edge							
O) every ___ rows ___ times	2/8	2/8	2/8	3/8	2/9	2/9	2/9
1/2 FRONT (Cardigan/Jkt)							
P) CO Straight Shape	23	24	26	27	29	30	32
P) CO Fingertip Taper	25	26	28	30	32	33	35
Q) Dec 1 at side edge every ___" ___ times	8.5/2	8.5/2	9/2	6/3	6.5/3	6/3	6/3
P) CO Long Taper	29	31	32	34	36	38	39
Q) Dec 1 at side edge every ___" ___ times	4.5/6	4/7	5/6	4/17	4/7	3.5/8	4/7
Round Neck Shaping							
R) BO ___ sts beg next row	3	3	3	3	4	4	4
Follow shaping (L, M, N) from above at neck edge only							
SLEEVES							
S) CO Long Sleeve	18	18	18	20	22	22	22
T) Inc 1 ea end every ___ rows ___ times	6/11	6/11	6/12	6/11	6/11	6/12	6/12
S) CO Short Sleeve	30	30	32	34	34	36	36
T) Inc 1 ea end every ___ rows ___ times	3/5	3/5	3/5	4/4	3/5	3/5	3/5
S) CO Cap Sleeve	36	36	38	38	40	42	42
T) Inc 1 ea end every ___ rows ___ times	3/2	3/2	3/2	3/2	3/2	3/2	3/2
CAP SHAPING							
Set In							
U) BO ___ sts beg next 2 rows	2	2	2	3	3	3	4
V) Dec 1 ea end EOR for ___"	4	4	4	4.5	4.5	4.5	5
Modified Drop							
W) BO ___ sts beg every row ___ times	2/14	2/14	2/14	2/14	2/14	2/16	2/16

44	46	48	50	52	54	56	58	60
66	70	72	76	78	82	84	88	90
60	62	66	68	70	74	76	80	82
16/3	13/4	15/3	13/4	13/4	13/4	13/4	13/4	13/4
72	76	80	82	86	88	92	94	98
6/3	6/3	5/4	6.5/3	5/4	6.5/3	5/4	6.5/3	5/4
82	86	88	92	94	98	102	106	108
3.5/8	3.5/8	3.5/8	3.5/8	3.5/8	4/8	3.5/9	3.5/9	3.5/9
5/2	5/2	6/2	6/2	4/4	5/4	5/4	6/6	6/6
5	6	6	6	6	6	6	6	6
5	5	5	6	5	5	6	5	6
4/2	5/2	5.5/2	6/2	6/2	4/4	4/4	5/4	5/4
6	7	7	7	7	7	7	7	8
7	8	7	8	9	9	10	11	12
26	26	28	28	28	30	30	30	30
10	10	10	10	10	10	10	12	12
2	2	2	2	2	2	2	2	2
2	2	2	2	2	2	2	2	2
1	1	1	2	2	2	2	2	2
4/10	4/10	4/10	4/11	4/11	4/11	4/11	4/12	4/12
2/10	2/10	2/10	2/11	2/11	2/11	2/11	2/12	2/12
33	35	36	38	39	41	42	44	45
36	38	40	41	43	44	46	47	49
6/3	6/3	5/4	6.5/3	5/4	6.5/3	5/4	6.5/3	5/4
41	43	44	46	47	49	51	53	54
3.5/8	3.5/8	3.5/8	3.5/8	3.5/8	4/8	3.5/9	3.5/9	3.5/9
5	5	5	5	5	5	5	6	6
24	24	24	26	26	28	28	28	30
6/12	6/12	6/12	6/12	6/13	6/12	6/13	6/13	7/12
38	40	40	42	42	42	44	46	46
3/5	4/4	5/4	5/4	4/5	4/5	4/5	5/4	5/4
44	46	46	48	48	48	48	50	50
3/2	4/1	6/1	6/1	4/2	4/2	4/3	5/2	5/2
4	5	5	6	6	4	4	5	5
5	5	5.5	5.5	5.5	6	6	6.5	6.5
2/16	2/16	2/16	2/16	2/16	2/16	3/14	3/14	3/14

Gauge *(2.5 sts x 3 rows = 1")*

Finished Bust/Chest	30	32	34	36	38	40	42
1/2 BODY (Back)							
A) CO Straight Body	38	40	42	46	48	50	54
A) CO Cropped Shape Taper	34	36	38	42	44	46	48
B) Inc 1 ea end every ___ rows ___ times	16/2	16/2	16/2	16/2	16/2	16/2	12/3
A) CO Fingertip Taper	42	44	46	50	52	54	60
C) Dec 1 ea end every ___" ___ times	8/2	8/2	8/2	8/2	8/2	8/2	6/3
A) CO Long Taper	48	50	54	58	60	62	66
C) Dec 1 ea end every ___" ___ times	6/5	6/5	5/6	5/6	5/6	5/6	5/6
SHAPE ARMHOLE							
Cut In (sleeveless)							
E) BO ___ sts beg next ___ rows	2/2	2/2	3/2	3/2	3/2	3/2	4/2
F) Dec 1 ea end EOR ___ times	2	3	3	3	4	4	4
G) Dec 1 ea end every 4th row ___ times	2	2	2	3	3	3	4
Set In							
E) BO ___ sts beg next ___ rows	2/2	2/2	2/2	2/2	2/2	3/2	3/2
F) Dec 1 ea end EOR ___ times	1	2	2	4	4	4	6
Modified Drop							
H) BO ___ sts beg next 2 rows	2	2	2	4	4	5	6
1/2 BODY (Pullover Front)							
Boatneck: (J) BO ctr ___ sts	20	20	20	20	22	22	22
Round Neck Shaping							
K) BO ctr ___ sts	6	6	6	6	6	6	6
L) BO ___ sts ea neck edge 1 time	2	2	2	2	2	2	2
M) BO ___ sts ea neck edge 1 time	0	0	0	0	0	0	2
N) Dec 1 ea neck edge EOR ___ times	1	1	2	2	2	2	1
Deep V: Dec ea neck edge							
O) every ___ rows ___ times	4/6	4/6	3/7	3/7	3/7	3/7	3/8
Shallow V: Dec ea neck edge							
O) every ___ rows ___ times	2/6	2/6	2/7	2/7	2/7	2/7	2/8
1/2 FRONT (Cardigan/Jkt)							
P) CO Straight Shape	19	20	21	23	24	25	27
P) CO Fingertip Taper	21	22	23	25	26	27	30
Q) Dec 1 at side edge every ___" ___ times	8/2	8/2	8/2	8/2	8/2	8/2	6/3
P) CO Long Taper	24	25	27	29	30	31	33
Q) Dec 1 at side edge every ___" ___ times	6/5	6/5	5/6	5/6	5/6	5/6	5/6
Round Neck Shaping							
R) BO ___ sts beg next row	3	3	3	3	3	3	3
Follow shaping (L, M, N) from above at neck edge only							
SLEEVES							
S) CO Long Sleeve	15	15	16	16	17	18	18
T) Inc 1 ea end every ___ rows ___ times	5/9	5/10	5/10	5/10	5/10	5/10	5/10
S) CO Short Sleeve	25	25	26	26	27	28	30
T) Inc 1 ea end every ___ rows ___ times	3/4	2/5	2/5	2/5	2/5	2/5	3/4
S) CO Cap Sleeve	29	31	32	32	33	34	36
T) Inc 1 ea end every ___ rows ___ times	2/2	2/2	2/2	2/2	2/2	2/2	4/1
CAP SHAPING							
Set In							
U) BO ___ sts beg next 2 rows	2	2	2	2	2	3	3
V) Dec 1 ea end EOR for ___"	4	4	4	4.5	4.5	4.5	5
Modified Drop							
W) BO ___ sts beg every row ___ times	2/10	2/10	2/10	2/10	2/10	2/10	3/10

44	46	48	50	52	54	56	58	60
56	58	60	62	66	68	70	72	76
50	52	54	56	58	60	62	64	68
12/3	12/3	12/3	12/3	10/4	10/4	10/4	10/4	10/4
62	64	66	68	74	76	78	80	84
6/3	6/3	6/3	6/3	5/4	5/4	5/4	5/4	5/4
68	72	74	76	80	82	86	88	92
5/6	4/7	4/7	4/7	4/7	4/7	4/8	4/8	4/8
5/2	5/2	4/4	4/4	4/4	5/4	5/4	4/4	4/4
4	4	3	4	4	4	4	3	4
4	4	3	3	4	3	3	3	3
3/2	3/2	3/2	3/2	2/4	2/4	3/4	3/4	3/4
6	7	7	7	8	8	7	7	8
7	6	6	6	8	8	9	9	10
22	22	22	24	24	24	24	26	26
6	6	6	6	6	6	6	6	6
2	2	2	2	3	3	3	3	3
2	2	2	2	2	2	2	2	2
1	1	1	1	1	1	1	1	1
3/8	3/8	3/8	3/8	3/9	3/9	3/9	3/9	3/9
2/8	2/8	2/8	2/8	2/9	2/9	2/9	2/9	2/9
28	29	30	31	33	34	35	36	38
31	32	33	34	37	38	39	40	42
6/3	6/3	6/3	6/3	5/4	5/4	5/4	5/4	5/4
34	36	37	38	40	41	43	44	46
5/6	4/7	4/7	4/7	4/7	4/7	4/8	4/8	4/8
3	3	3	3	3	3	3	3	3
20	20	20	20	22	22	22	24	24
5/10	5/10	5/10	5/10	5/10	5/10	5/11	5/11	5/11
32	32	32	34	34	36	36	38	38
3/4	3/4	4/4	4/4	4/4	4/4	4/4	4/4	4/4
38	38	38	40	40	40	40	40	40
4/1	4/1	4/1	6/1	6/1	6/1	4/2	3/3	3/3
3	3	3	3	3	3	3	3	3
5	5	5.5	5.5	5.5	6	6	6.5	6.5
3/10	3/10	3/10	3/10	3/10	3/10	3/12	3/12	3/12

Gauge *(2 sts x 3 rows = 1")*

Finished Bust/Chest	30	32	34	36	38	40	42
1/2 BODY (Back)							
A) CO Straight Body	30	32	34	36	38	40	42
A) CO Cropped Shape Taper	26	28	30	32	34	36	38
B) Inc 1 ea end every ___ rows ___ times	14/2	14/2	14/2	14/2	14/2	14/2	14/2
A) CO Fingertip Taper	34	36	38	40	42	44	46
C) Dec 1 ea end every ___" ___ times	8/2	8/2	8/2	8/2	8/2	9/2	9/2
A) CO Long Taper	38	40	44	46	48	50	52
C) Dec 1 ea end every ___" ___ times	6/4	6/4	6/5	6/5	6/5	6/5	6/5
SHAPE ARMHOLE							
Cut In (sleeveless)							
E) BO ___ sts beg next ___ rows	2/2	2/2	2/2	2/2	2/2	3/2	3/2
F) Dec 1 ea end EOR ___ times	1	1	2	2	3	3	4
G) Dec 1 ea end every 4th row ___ times	1	1	1	2	2	2	2
Set In							
E) BO ___ sts beg next ___ rows	2/2	2/2	2/2	2/2	2/2	2/2	2/2
F) Dec 1 ea end EOR ___ times	1	1	2	2	3	4	5
Modified Drop							
H) BO ___ sts beg next 2 rows	2	2	2	3	3	4	4
1/2 BODY (Pullover Front)							
Boatneck: (J) BO ctr ___ sts	16	16	16	16	18	18	18
Round Neck Shaping							
K) BO ctr ___ sts	4	4	4	4	4	4	4
L) BO ___ sts ea neck edge 1 time	2	2	2	2	2	2	2
M) BO ___ sts ea neck edge 1 time	0	0	0	0	0	0	0
N) Dec 1 ea neck edge EOR ___ times	1	1	1	1	2	2	2
Deep V: Dec ea neck edge							
O) every ___ rows ___ times	4/5	4/5	4/5	4/5	4/6	4/6	4/6
Shallow V: Dec ea neck edge							
O) every ___ rows ___ times	2/5	2/5	2/5	2/5	2/6	2/6	2/6
1/2 FRONT (Cardigan/Jkt)							
P) CO Straight Shape	15	16	17	18	19	20	21
P) CO Fingertip Taper	17	18	19	20	21	22	23
Q) Dec 1 at side edge every ___" ___ times	8/2	8/2	8/2	8/2	8/2	9/2	9/2
P) CO Long Taper	19	20	22	23	24	25	26
Q) Dec 1 at side edge every ___" ___ times	6/4	6/4	6/5	6/5	6/5	6/5	6/5
Round Neck Shaping							
R) BO ___ sts beg next row	2	2	2	2	2	2	2
Follow shaping (L, M, N) from above at neck edge only							
SLEEVES							
S) CO Long Sleeve	12	12	12	14	14	14	14
T) Inc 1 ea end every ___ rows ___ times	6/7	6/7	6/8	7/6	8/6	6/8	6/8
S) CO Short Sleeve	20	20	22	22	22	24	24
T) Inc 1 ea end every ___ rows ___ times	3/3	3/3	3/3	3/3	4/3	4/3	4/3
S) CO Cap Sleeve	24	24	26	26	26	28	28
T) Inc 1 ea end every ___ rows ___ times	3/1	3/1	3/1	3/1	4/1	4/1	4/1
CAP SHAPING							
Set In							
U) BO ___ sts beg next 2 rows	2	2	2	2	2	2	2
V) Dec 1 ea end EOR for ___"	4	4	4	4.5	4.5	4.5	5
Modified Drop							
W) BO ___ sts beg every row ___ times	2/10	2/10	2/10	2/10	2/10	2/10	2/10

44	46	48	50	52	54	56	58	60
44	46	48	50	52	54	56	58	60
40	40	43	44	46	48	50	52	54
14/2	10/3	10/3	10/3	10/3	10/3	10/3	10/3	10/3
48	52	54	56	58	60	62	64	66
9/2	6/3	6/3	6/3	6/3	7/3	7/3	7/3	7/3
54	56	58	60	64	66	68	70	72
6/5	6/5	6/5	6/5	5/6	5/6	5/6	5/6	5/6
3/2	2/4	3/4	3/4	3/4	3/4	3/4	3/4	3/4
5	5	4	4	6	7	9	9	10
2	2	2	2	1	1	0	0	0
2/2	3/2	3/2	3/2	3/2	3/2	3/2	3/2	3/2
5	5	5	5	6	7	8	8	9
5	5	5	5	6	6	7	7	8
18	18	18	20	20	20	20	20	20
4	4	4	4	4	4	4	4	4
2	2	2	2	2	2	2	2	2
0	0	2	2	2	2	2	2	2
2	2	1	1	1	1	1	1	1
4/6	4/6	3/7	3/7	3/7	3/7	4/7	4/7	4/7
2/6	2/6	2/6	2/7	2/7	2/7	2/7	2/7	2/7
22	23	24	25	26	27	28	29	30
24	26	27	28	29	30	31	32	33
9/2	6/3	6/3	6/3	6/3	7/3	7/3	7/3	7/3
27	28	29	30	32	33	34	35	36
6/5	6/5	6/5	6/5	5/6	5/6	5/6	5/6	5/6
2	2	2	2	2	2	2	2	2
15	16	16	17	18	18	18	18	18
6/8	6/8	6/8	6/8	6/8	6/8	6/9	6/9	6/9
25	26	26	27	28	28	30	30	30
4/3	4/3	4/3	4/3	4/3	4/3	4/3	4/3	4/3
29	30	30	31	32	32	32	32	32
4/1	4/1	4/1	4/1	4/1	4/1	3/2	3/2	3/2
2	3	3	3	3	3	3	3	3
5	5	5.5	5.5	5.5	6	6	6.5	6.5
2 /10	3/10	3/10	3/10	3/10	3/10	3/10	3/10	3/10

ABBREVIATIONS AND GLOSSARY

cn	cable needle
garter st	garter stitch: back and forth, knit every round; in the round, knit one row and purl one row
K	knit
K2tog	knit two stitches together—one stitch decreased
M1	make one—one stitch increased
P	purl
P2tog	purl two stitches together—one stitch decreased
rep	repeat
RS	right side
sl st	slip stitch as if to purl, with yarn in back unless specified otherwise
sl 1-K2-psso	slip one stitch as if to knit, knit two stitches, pass slipped stitch over—one stitch decreased
sl 1-K2tog-psso	slip one stitch as if to knit, knit two stitches together, pass slipped stitch over—two stitches decreased
sl 2-K1-p2sso	slip two stitches together as if to knit, knit one stitch, pass two slipped stitches over together—two stitches decreased
ssk	slip slip, knit: slip two stitches as if to knit, one at a time, insert left needle into front loops and knit two stitches together—one stitch decreased
St st	stockinette stitch: back and forth, knit on right side, purl on wrong side; in the round, knit every round
st(s)	stitch(es)
wyib	with yarn in back
wyif	with yarn in front
WS	wrong side
YO	yarn over

ABOUT THE AUTHORS

Laura Militzer Bryant

Laura Militzer Bryant discovered her passion for fibers at an early age. She began knitting as a child, received a Bachelor of Fine Arts from the University of Michigan, and worked in retail knitting and as a sales representative for several knitting yarn companies after college. In 1984 Laura took the plunge and founded her company, Prism Arts, Inc.

Laura's design excellence has been recognized with individual artist grants from both the National Endowment for the Arts and the state of Florida. She has published more than 55 pattern books for Prism Arts, and has been featured in *Vogue, Knitter's, Cast On,* and *Love of Knitting* where she writes a regular column, "Ask Laura." She teaches design and knitting techniques at conventions, stores, and retreats around the country. Laura is past president of the National Needlearts Association, and recipient of the Tribute to Excellence in Needlearts award, bestowed by her peers in recognition of her contributions to the knitting industry.

Barry Klein

Growing up, *Barry Klein* spent afternoons in his mother's retail needlework store. Once he got his hands on yarn, he was forever addicted. While earning a marketing and film degree in college, he worked as a sweater and yarn designer for Fantacia, one of the first fashion yarn companies.

Barry and his mother, Myrna, started Trendsetter Yarns, staying true to their passions for bringing the most exciting fashion yarns and the most luxurious classic yarns to the knitting market. Barry has taught extensively at knitting conventions, in store exhibits, and on knitting cruises. A past president of the National Needlework Association, he has created patterns and written articles for *Vogue Knitting, Knitters, Knit 'N Style, Love of Knitting,* and *Cast On* magazines as well as been a featured talent on knitting shows Uncommon Threads, Needleart Studio, Knitty Gritty, and Knitting Daily. Barry was recently featured in "Top 10 Men in Knitting," an article on Knitty.com (Winter 2009) that profiled the 10 most influential men in the world of knitting.

There's More Online!

Learn more about Laura's yarns, designs, and passion for color at www.prismyarn.com. Explore Barry's extensive yarn and pattern lines at www.trendsetteryarns.com. Find more great books on knitting, crochet, and more at www.martingale-pub.com.

You might also enjoy these other fine titles from

MARTINGALE & COMPANY

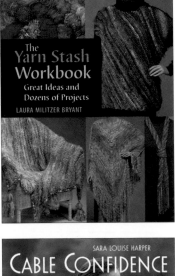

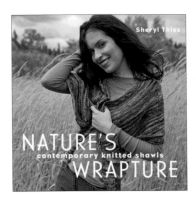

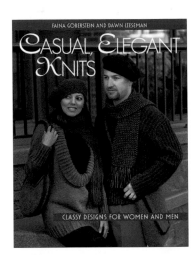

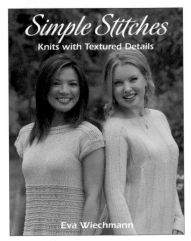